An
Accidental
Novelist

A Literary Memoir

An Accidental Novelist

A Literary Memoir

Richard S. Wheeler

SUNSTONE
PRESS

SANTA FE

Sunstone books may be purchased for educational, business, or sales
promotional use. For information please write: Special Markets Department,
Sunstone Press, P.O. Box 2321, Santa Fe, New Mexico 87504-2321.

Library of Congress Cataloging-in-Publication Data

Wheeler, Richard S.
  An accidental novelist : a literary memoir / Richard S. Wheeler.
      p. cm.
  Includes bibliographical references (p.   )
   ISBN 978-0-86534-562-1 (alk. paper) -- ISBN 978-0-86534-563-8 (pbk. : alk.
paper)
 1. Wheeler, Richard S. 2. Novelists, American--20th century--Biography. 3. West
(U.S.)--In literature. I. Title.

PS3573.H4345Z46 2007
813'.54--dc22
[B]
                                    2007005316

Published in

WWW.SUNSTONEPRESS.COM
SUNSTONE PRESS / POST OFFICE BOX 2321 / SANTA FE, NM 87504-2321 /USA
(505) 988-4418 / ORDERS ONLY (800) 243-5644 / FAX (505) 988-1025

To those I have loved,
and especially those who never knew it.

1

The Pundit

HERE I AM A NOVELIST. WHO WOULD HAVE IMAGINED IT? Certainly not anyone who knew me during my first forty years. By some mysterious process I ended up a storyteller, and I did it while clinging to the mast of a sinking ship. I have written sixty western and historical novels for such publishers as Doubleday, Forge, Ballantine, Fawcett, Bantam, Pinnacle, Signet, Walker and Company, M. Evans and Sunstone. Add a few short stories to that. I have received various awards along the way, and more favorable reviews than I can remember. I've had a handful of unfavorable ones that I remember all too well.

It was not my youthful intention to write fiction. I had settled on journalism as a vocation, and hoped some-day to become a pundit. That would be a fine life. I would wear horn-rimmed glasses, a tweed jacket and a bow tie, and impress the world with my erudition and wisdom. I would live happily in some noble manse, and two or three times a week I would wire my wisdom to a metropolitan paper such as *The New York Times*, or *Washington Post*, or *Wall Street Journal*. I would be married to an elegant and wise woman, entertain important people at my dinner table, study the day's news as it arrived by teletype in my private study, and then I would whip out my columns and hand them to a little twit who would hasten to the nearest telegraph office. And I would enjoy the fruits of my wisdom: a fine salary, a secure position, the pleasure of influencing national politics and public policy, and of course, an award or two, maybe even a Pulitzer.

Richard Wheeler, the Pundit. The next Scotty Reston. The next Walter Lippmann. I had all sorts of opinions to peddle. I read all the pundits. I knew how to write the studied opinion, the oblique criticism, the startling insight, the gracious concession. I knew the names of all the nation's pundits. I could tell you all about Tom Wicker or Anthony Lewis and what they thought. I could tell you what William F. Buckley was thinking.

At least I was ambitious. Young people are certain they know what's what and what's right, and that went double for me. But a funny thing happened en route to becoming a great pundit. I kept getting fired. I lasted only a year or so at the *Phoenix Gazette*, an afternoon daily no longer in existence. That was my first career job. I was toiling on the editorial pages, editing letters and syndicated columns, learning how to stuff them into holes on the page that were invariably smaller than the material I was dealing with.

I spent a lot of time inhaling smoke down in that grubby composing room, surrounded by clattering linotype machines and compositors in grimy aprons who would stuff the type into the holes in the page forms. Then they ran off a gummy page proof which it was my duty to correct, and heaven help me if I let some typos slide by. I enjoyed the pungence of hot lead and black ink, and even now it evokes pleasant nostalgia in me and most anyone else who labored on papers during the hot-lead era. The typesetters and compositors and stereotypers and pressmen all had their separate skills, and were the elite of the trade-union world, and worthy of respect. And if they sometimes needled a green youth, which they did, it was only to let that youth know that journalism and printing were not vocations that could be mastered by any fool off the streets. They were like wise old master sergeants having some gentle fun with some poor shavetail lieutenant.

I had landed that job largely as the result of writing a popular Henry Mencken-type column for the University of Wisconsin campus newspaper, *The Daily Cardinal*. In it, I diligently insulted and offended as many people and groups as possible, and gauged the success of each column by the number of howling letters that would flood into the offices of the student paper. These columns caught the attention of a publisher named Gene Pulliam, and won me an unusual opening job: I began my journalism career not as a cub reporter, learning the news business from the ground up, but as an editorial page assistant.

Once in a while the *Gazette*'s editor, Ed Fitzhugh, would even let me write an editorial. I remember writing an obituary editorial for Ernest Hemingway. It was hollow because I knew little about him and had read little of his fiction. That meant I had to cull my information from the obituaries that were arriving on the chattering teletypes. I should have learned something then, but I didn't: you don't venture opinions, especially public ones, without a thorough knowledge of what you're opining about. It was a superficial look at the author's life and work.

But that didn't deter a young man in his twenties, blissfully proceeding ahead on a fast-track to punditry and fame. Wasn't the world grand? Wasn't sleepy little Phoenix the most delightful place on earth? Wasn't my new wife, my college partner in crime, Rita Middleton, sweet and funny and wicked? Wasn't Scottsdale a paradise? Wasn't Arizona magical? We honeymooned in Oak Creek

Canyon and I returned to the editorial pages, thinking the world was my auditorium. Shortly after we had been married the publisher invited us to a soiree at a Phoenix hotel honoring Clare Boothe Luce, who was thin, gray-haired, and striking. We were introduced to the great lady as newlyweds. She eyed us shrewdly from her perch on the velveteen divan, and said she was sure we deserved each other. That was a classic Boothean remark, which I still cherish.

Then one day, out of the blue, Ed Fitzhugh summoned me to his sanctum. The conversation went something like this:

"You know," he said, "you've started near the top of the profession, and it was our mistake. Your job is usually given to someone who's put in years of reporting and maybe some editing in the newsroom. I'm sorry we started you at this level. The problem is, you're writing and editing without a proper background. You have some abstract book knowledge but you don't know how the world works. You simply haven't lived long enough. A few years as a beat reporter, writing up stories about politics, public affairs, births and deaths, obituaries, and all the rest of it, would have given you the seasoning you need."

He handed me an envelope.

"Here's a check for two weeks. We're letting you go. I'm sorry things didn't work out. I'll be glad to recommend you for another job, as long as it's at the level where you can begin to absorb this profession. You have some skills, and you worked hard, but you're not ready to work on an opinion page."

Fired.

I stumbled out of that office, bumbled down the marble-ized stair to the front door of the newspaper, stepped into the hot desert air, and found myself staring at the tan fortress that had just ejected me. I walked the block a couple of times, and then returned to an alien building to collect my stuff. Ed Fitzhugh was right. He also was wise, and had charitably given me a long time to prove myself, which I never did. The young Richard Wheeler didn't know how the real world worked, and his editorials weren't exactly astute.

There was nothing to do but clean out my desk and leave. I stopped to tell my friend Ed McDowell, over on the morning paper, the *Arizona Republic*, of my demise as an employee of Phoenix Newspapers. He and his wife Carol and Rita and I had become friends. Ed eventually landed at the *Wall Street Journal* and then *The New York Times*.

It was harder to tell Rita. She had gotten a job she enjoyed as a publicist with a Phoenix playhouse, and now everything would change. I would have to find work elsewhere. We would have to give up our honeymoon apartment on Thomas Road, near the Phoenix Country Club. We would have to find jobs and start all over again.

Fired. She eyed me gravely. She had her own humor, which consisted of thinking up the most startling and outrageous things that could be said about anything. But this time she said nothing.

I could detail a downward-spiraling career in journalism here, but it is not necessary. I want to explore how I ended up a novelist against my better judgment. Suffice it to say I worked several more papers, with more or less ignominious results. Surprisingly, I ended up on the editorial pages of the *Oakland Tribune* a bounce or two after my hasty exit from Phoenix, and there I survived for several years. That paper occupied an old tower in downtown Oakland, with ancient oak desks that had been scalloped with cigaret burns. Its editors wore green eye shades. The stink of long-dead cigars permeated the whole place, even the paint on the walls. Some of the editors had a hootch problem, but so did most of the news staff at the *Tribune*. The wire editor, who had a doctoral degree, was effective only around eleven each morning. His task was to select and paste together the foreign news stories from rival AP and UP wire services, and he had only a brief window each morning in which to do it. It required several screwdrivers for him to reach functionality and stitch together the international news, but one screwdriver too many meant that the *Tribune* would publish no foreign news that day. It was a fine line, but he usually got the work out before lapsing into afternoon delirium.

My editorial page editor, Jack Ryan, was famous for asking Marilyn Monroe what she wore to bed, which turned out to be Chanel Number Five. I arrived one morning to find him stretched out on a work table. I couldn't arouse him and his moribund snooze was making me very nervous. I decided to wait, and circled the block a few times, getting up courage to call for a hearse, but when I returned he had vanished. He resigned soon after, and I found myself editing the opinion pages. So there I was, a genuine pundit at age 28, and the youngest editorial page editor of a metro paper in the country. I had more or less reached my goal in life.

Rita had gotten a job writing advertising copy in a local agency, and fell for one of her employers. They went off on business trips all the time, and I was too dumb to figure out what sort of business. I just kept on adoring her. She had started at the University of Wisconsin at age fifteen, part of a Ford Foundation experiment to accelerate the education of the very bright. School was a snap for her; but coping with the University of Wisconsin's adult life and readily available 3.2 percent beer was another matter. She was tall, beautiful, funny and wicked, and after a few years in Oakland she divorced me. I abandoned the *Tribune*; it hurt too much to hang around Oakland. Eventually she married the guy, and later divorced him, lost her marbles, was institutionalized, and then she died in 1984 at age forty-four of lung cancer. Sometimes deep in the night I remember her and have a conversation with her. She still has that wicked smile.

A few more journalist jobs followed. I worked for *Reader's Digest* in Washington D.C., ensconced in its elegant offices off Dupont Circle. These were as unlike the Oakland editorial offices as could be, with oriental rugs, gleaming desks with inlaid leather, hunt etchings on the walls, and lush leather furnishings. I lasted only a few months, though I did meet several genuine Washington D. C. pundits, and basked in their wisdom. But alas for me, I remained in a funk about losing Rita, and one day they found me at my desk, tears on my cheeks, semi-coherent.

I was long gone from my Wisconsin family, but my parents took me in. It took a while to get past Rita, but I did.

More newspaper jobs followed: the *Billings Gazette*, the *Nevada-Appeal* in Carson City, the *Billings Gazette* a second time, and briefly, the *Press-Gazette* in Green Bay. I was a general assignment reporter at the beck and call of assorted Napoleonic city editors, and I was discovering that I wasn't much good at it. It requires some brass to be a good reporter, and I am a born wimp. In spite of all that, I somehow won a major journalism award. It was from the American Political Science Association honoring me for "distinguished reporting of public affairs." A series on air pollution, written long before it became a national issue, won it for me.

That was during the Vietnam war, a fight that intruded every day upon the newsrooms of the world. In Billings I had written a story about an army sergeant who was returning to Nam for his third tour. A few months later the wire came to the *Gazette*: the guy had been killed in action. A telegram went simultaneously to his widow, announcing the death. That's how things were done in those times.

The city editor summoned me. "Wheeler, call her up and get a reaction story."

A reaction story. Call the widow up and get her reaction and write it up. Just dial the lady. I returned to my bullpen desk knowing it was beyond me, and the city editor was a monster.

"Mrs. Jones, how do you feel about your husband getting shot? Will you miss him? What will your children think? Do you favor the war? Is this Richard Nixon's fault?"

I sat at my desk unable to make that call. I stared at the phone, knowing absolutely I could not make my fingers twirl that dial. I also knew that if I disobeyed the City Desk Napoleon who popped reporters hither and yon like yo-yos on a string, I'd better start looking for another job. Eleven o'clock was looming. That was the deadline for the afternoon edition, and my deadline for that story, and I still couldn't manage it. But at about two minutes to eleven, knowing my job hung in balance, I forced my fingers to turn that dial. Click, click, and then ring, ring. Thank heaven, the woman's mother had arrived and took the call, and I managed to croak out a few questions. Yes, she said, the widow had received word. She was in seclusion. She was torn to pieces. Her mother would be there with her.

I thanked the mother for confirming the news, and wrote the story, thin as it was, hating the city editor, hating journalism, hating newspapers in general and specifically the *Gazette*. I suppose that editor was typical. He belonged to one party; the local politicians belonged to the other, and he saw his opportunity. Prior to an election, he assigned me to do candidate stories on them all, and "cut their throats." That is a request I have never forgotten. I didn't obey him because I refused to do any throat-cutting in the news columns. Throat-cutting is reserved for the opinion pages. Each candidate was written up as accurately as I knew how, and in fact a few of them cut their own throats with no help from me.

I won a few best-story-of-the-month awards at the *Gazette*, but even so I wasn't good at it. The ideal reporter swiftly develops rapport with the people he interviews. Contrary to the notions about reporting that emerged during the Watergate period, good reporters are rarely adversarial. The best stories rise from a reporter's innate curiosity and carefully cultivated sources. Some stories I wrote well; others, especially in the realm of politics, or getting material from public officials, I was not very good at and the stories were thin. I gradually understood that these deficiencies went to the core of my being because I am non-confrontational.

I sought to change my career track to editing, and hoped that I could be a good newspaper editor. For a while I did succeed as an assistant city editor, but the editorial ladder at any paper is wrought with politics, and eventually I got bumped back to reporting to make room for a hotshot kid out of the Medill School of Journalism at Northwestern University who was going to the top and was being groomed to be a publisher in that newspaper chain.

I had scraped together enough to buy a half-section of Montana land north of Billings, in dry country called the Bull Mountains. I paid $39 an acre, or $12,500 in all, on a contract for deed. It had hay meadows, a couple of springs, a stock well, serrated tan sandstone cliffs, and a lot of jack pine. There I lived in a weathered log cabin, learned how to raise and ride horses, and how to enjoy rural life in a rural state. I loved that place, and thought I had my very own piece of the West, which I would keep forever. I had lots of visitors, and rented pasture to some people at the *Gazette*, which resulted in great riding at least in the summer months. I more or less turned myself into a horseman, wore Levi jeans, boots, cowboy hats, and pretended I knew what I was doing.

But after I had been shifted back to reporting, I didn't do well, and eventually got axed by an ambitious new editor. He was an urban fellow full of journalism school notions, who once came to my ranch in Bermuda shorts and sneakers, and just barely escaped being bitten by a prairie rattler. If I had not yelled at him, he would have taken the fangs right in his hairy calf. He did a sideways arabesque, thanked me profusely, and within a few months, he and the managing editor fired me. Newspapering is like that. The guy ended up a publisher out in Oregon. I walked away from the *Billings Gazette* knowing a chapter had ended, and seeing little future at all.

So there I was, in midlife, knowing my journalistic career was over, and I had utterly no employment prospects in that field. Too many hirings and firings. I was single, too. I had a few romances, but nothing serious. I couldn't make payments on my

Montana paradise, and had to sell it. I made a little on the sale, enough to keep me afloat for a year, anyway. But what to do? I sure didn't know.

2

The Editor

THE WORTHIES WHO HAD BOOTED ME FROM THE *GAZETTE* HAD DONE ME A FAVOR, but it was years before I understood that. That was more or less the end of my career as a newsman. To be sure, I immediately flooded most of the dailies in the United States, except for the abominable South, with my résumé, which did have some impressive facets to it. But it all came to nothing. All those hirings and firings, and probably some negative words from the gentlemen who had axed me put an end to my newspaper career.

So much for punditry. What else might I do? Indeed, how could I feed my face? Go back to college, learn some vocation? I knew I was in deep trouble in the middle of my life, and I also knew I had no answers. But eventually I was rescued by a friend, Jameson Campaigne, Jr, who was the son of the editor of *Indianapolis Star*, one of Gene Pulliam's papers. Jameson was the director of a new division of Open Court Publishing Company, of La Salle, Illinois. The venerable company had been around for generations and was the foremost American publisher of philosophers, including Albert Einstein, Jean-Paul Sartre, Karl Popper, Carl Jung, and others of note. The Carus family, which owned the company, had been patrons of philosophy and high scholarship for a century, and had devoted much of their income from their chemical company to underwriting scholarship. In recent years they had added a textbook division, devoted to teaching young people to read better. And they were publishing *Cricket Magazine* for children. When I arrived, they had started a new trade book division devoted to serious discussion of issues, but for a general readership rather than academics. It would be similar to Basic Books, and its editorial board would encompass some of the most distinguished intellectuals of those days.

I settled in La Salle, eager to tackle this challenging new field. La Salle was a nondescript town on the Illinois River, surrounded by some of the best farmland in the world, which was devoted entirely to corn and soybeans. It was flat and unprepossessing. In the summertime, the roads from La Salle carved their way through walls of ten-foot-high corn. It wasn't where my heart sang, but it was a good job in the world of ideas and public affairs. I loved the work. There I was, editing material intended to last for generations, unlike news stories that would line the bottom of bird cages the next day. I yearned for the western life I had come to love in Arizona and Montana, but this job was a paradise in itself. I was well paid and found myself working on books by well-known scholars. Some of these people flew in for editorial conferences, and I enjoyed dinners and lunches with men and women of great intellect. The line included books by Melvin Lasky, editor of *Encounter* Magazine, Sidney Hook, Nobel Prize-winning economist Milton Friedman, and others at that level.

So I lived in the world of ideas, worked hard, and gradually reconciled myself to central Illinois, in fact finding amiable people and new friends there. There were other advantages. I wasn't far away from Milwaukee and my widowed mother, and I was able to drive up there regularly and see my family. The new trade book division was costing the Carus family a lot of money, but the books were impressive and if all went well it would break even in a few years.

On one occasion we all headed to New York for a sales conference, which was to be in the Algonquin Hotel. The thought of staying at the famous literary hotel delighted me, and when I arrived I explored those famous precincts where the most engaging wits in the country had regularly met at the round table.

I had grown up with *The New Yorker*. I had blotted up the entire legendry of the Algonquin round table, and those bright lights whose crackling wit and humor had become an American legend. As soon as I was settled in my room, I headed downstairs for those precincts where so much literary history had occurred. In the early seventies, these were barren and forlorn, but even in its faded glory, the Algonquin remained the heart and soul of American literature and theater, and my imagination supplied what was missing.

For there, indeed, through the twenties and thirties, the brightest and most entertaining journalists and theater people and writers collected for lunch. There were Harold Ross, the high school dropout and AWOL soldier who became the founder of *The New Yorker*, Robert Benchley, the managing editor of *Vanity Fair*; Heywood Broun and his wife Ruth Hale, who was *The New York Times*'s first female reporter, the incomparable Dorothy Parker, and drama critic Alexander Woollcott, whose wit survives him to this day. And of course Woollcott had been transformed into Sheridan Whiteside, the central figure in the play, *The Man Who Came to Dinner*. There were more: playwright George S. Kaufman and his wife, Beatrice. Playwright Marc Connelly, comedian Harpo Marx, and novelist Edna Ferber.

There were enough Pulitzer prizes in that group to hand

out one apiece and have some left over. I stood there in the deep quiet, in a nondescript autumn afternoon, not far from the lobby and its cigar stand, letting that world seep through me. They were long gone, those wits and raconteurs. The last meeting of the round table occurred in 1943 in the middle of the war, when I was eight. But the legend lives, in the modern *New Yorker* and *Vanity Fair*, and in a hundred books, plays, novels, and newspaper stories.

I knew where my love of that place, and that group, had come from. My mother had been an English teacher. I had read the works of many of these authors in high school, or had seen their plays. My father was a patent attorney, and the magazines arriving at our home included *Scientific American*, and *Popular Mechanics*, all of which I devoured along with the literary magazines such as *The New Yorker* or *American Heritage*, as well as *The Saturday Evening Post, Look, Life, Time*, and many others. I know now that my parents subscribed to a wide variety of magazines to foster their children's education and acquaint us with the varieties of life. Maybe if a high school dropout like Harold Ross could found the most delightful of all magazines, there would be hope for me.

I had, without quite realizing it, fashioned my life upon the round table. Benchley and Woollcott and Broun and Ross were my mentors; during my marriage, Rita was my Dorothy Parker, and full of the same wild humor. If the ghosts of those people had gathered once again at that table, this time with me, I would have felt utterly at home. More than that, I would have felt that I belonged.

The Open Court sales conference went smoothly, and soon I was back at my editing duties in the corn flats of Illinois. It was a life. I was back in the world of public policy and intellectuals rather than literature, but I didn't forget how my heart sang at the Algonquin. I was a resident of Illinois now, an editor of intellectuals, and that was how my life would play out–except for the oil shocks of the early seventies, when the Arabs turned off the spigots. Those were the times when people waited in long lines to get gasoline, if there was any to get; five gallons was the most the filling station attendants would dole out; you dared not drive cross country without a few jerry cans of reserve gasoline. And the prices of gasoline began a rise that continues even now.

The awful reality is that only a few years after I had found a new vocation as a book editor, I found myself on the streets once again. The oil shocks produced the severe recession of 1973 and 1974. Editors and reporters were once again laid off by the thousands. The Carus family's bankers, worried about all the red ink being spilled by the fledgling trade book division, which was years away from break-even, recommended that the company ditch the project. And so they did. The recession put financial strain on the whole Open Court Publishing company, and not just the new division. I was laid off. It was no consolation that I hadn't been fired. I was jobless again, and there were tens of thousands of book and newspaper editors and reporters who were in the same pickle. And there was no hope of a quick recovery, not until the nation's fuel supplies could be stabilized and alternatives to Arabian oil had been developed.

I had purchased a small rural house, which I then sold at a small rural profit, so I was not in critical need. But the sands were running through the hourglass, and I would either find a way to make a living in my field or end up in a low-level job. I have no objections to humble employment. In my day I've worked on a factory assembly line, delivered stoves and refrigerators for an appliance store, and worked as a clerk in a record store. It appeared that would be my fate.

But if I was no longer moored to Illinois, at least I could return to the West, and in particular, Arizona, where my heart always sang and my spirit was at peace. I loaded up my pickup truck, and headed west along with a Siamese cat I had acquired, and ended up at a guest ranch called Rancho de la Osa, located on the Mexican border southwest of Tucson, near a hamlet called Sasabe. The rancho was snugged into a shallow valley in the Sonoran desert, and was among the oldest in Arizona. It was once the seat of a Spanish land grant that included the whole Altar Valley, which stretched deep into Sonora and north virtually to Tucson. Some of the adobe buildings were ancient and were designated Arizona historical landmarks. Now it was owned by the Hamlin family of Boston, who operated it as a choice Sonora Desert guest ranch, carefully preserving the buildings and tradition of the old rancho.

One day I met one of the rancho's neighbors, Carlos Escalante, who lived in Sasabe and possessed the original La Osa Grant given by the Bourbon kings of Spain and scripted in Spanish so archaic that Carlos had to have it translated. He showed the ancient parchment to me, and I marveled that the hand-written script could be so elegantly formed, every letter and word as uniform as if it had been printed.

In years past La Osa had become a favorite hangout of Democratic politicians, and especially Justice William O. Douglas. It was famed as a bird watchers' paradise, and for its marvelous horse trails that wended through rough Sonoran desert, amid giant saguaro cactus, ocotillo, mesquite, and paloverde trees. During the winter guest season, wranglers took guests on morning and afternoon rides, or sometimes all-day rides through a desert wilderness. The place had a rich history, and until the 1950s, guests could ride into old Mexico, or participate in the border crossings, when corriente cattle were admitted to the United States and the day would end with a great fiesta. But the borders closed, and by the time I arrived, riding was confined to the United States side. But there was ample wilderness to ride in. I soon became a wrangler and took guests on lengthy trips through an indescribably idyllic Sonoran desert. Guests wondered how I could ride so well, and I did not tell them it was not due to any skill on my part, but because I had choice horses for my mounts.

Other times Border Patrol aircraft would zoom overhead because the remote Altar Valley was a great highway for illegal Mexican immigration. I loved that mysterious, empty land along the border, and soon was absorbed in its lore and history. By then the Altar Valley had become an established avenue for drug smugglers, but smuggling was nothing new to the border, and often the smuggling was southbound.

The border itself was simply a four-strand barbed-wire fence erected by American ranchers, and it had ordinary wire gates in it to facilitate the return of stray cattle, which customs and border officials carefully ignored. At times I would discover a stray corriente, the little Mexican cattle that did well on the desert, and soon enough a vaquero would ride up and take it back across the line. Off to the west were rough tan ridges, and to the north, the brooding blue spike of Baboquivari, piercing the heavens like an upraised loaf of bread. It was a mysterious land, and the little valleys often contained the ruins of a settlement or a few Hispanic graves. Some were still protected with a wrought-iron fence, but most of them were guarded by a tumbled-down picket fence trampled by cattle. The names of the dead were lost. Those settlers were long gone, driven out by the harsh desert or by loneliness. Reaching Rancho de la Osa required a seventy mile dirt-road drive, and sometimes when the arroyos were running there was no good way to get from the ranch to Tucson .

It was there that I found an odd, but delightful home. The manager, Mike Green, let me stay after the guest season in one of the little adobe casas, with its beehive fireplace in the corner for mesquite-log heat if I needed it. I still had to make a living, and jobs in book publishing were still scarce, especially for someone with only a few years of book editing behind him. I had, on occasion, sent out résumés and tried to track down jobs, to no avail. The applications were round-filed in distant offices, and I never received a reply. The publishing world didn't know that I existed.

My reserves from the sale of my Illinois house were dwindling. I was drifting closer to starvation with each passing week. I grew lethargic in the hot Sonoran summer. A job eluded me. My sporadic attempts at freelance editing netted me very little. I was lonely. The world was defeating me. I had ended up in one of the most remote corners of the United States, and was seeing my life slide by in emptiness. While I was welcome to stay for free at the guest ranch, I was steadily spending the last of my cash on food, maintaining my old pickup truck, and insurance. I did not even have cash enough to leave, or head toward publishing centers and seek editorial jobs.

It's not that life in Sasabe was uninteresting or that I lacked friends. The sheer remoteness of the place was an attraction to a certain sort, the odd adventuresome person who enjoyed living on the fringes of the civilized world. There were two or three more or less permanent people employed at the guest ranch, looking after the livestock and property. They were young and unattached and knew horses and were drifting, like myself. I met some of the Immigration, Customs and Border Patrol people stationed at the port of Sasabe, and some became friends. I could adventure into old Mexico, shop in the Sonoran hamlet of Sasabe, buy Mexican unrefined sugar, vanilla, and coffee there. I could venture up the long dirt road to Tucson now and then for groceries and relief from isolation. Once in a while there were cattle crossings, and truck-loads of little Mexican corriente cattle were run through troughs of vile-smelling dip that was supposed to kill all the bugs in the hides of those cattle, and sometimes killed the cattle for good measure if they swallowed some of it. But the days were long gone when these events ended with a fiesta, and people from both sides of the border enjoying cervezas and laughter.

A year passed, one I can't entirely remember except for the deepening sense of failure that was stealing through me. I did get an occasional freelance assignment. My friend Ed McDowell, now with the *Wall Street Journal*, had me write a piece about the remoteness of Sasabe. I was heartened by earning a few bucks, but nothing much changed. A neighbor, Elizabeth Brown Isaman, owned the neighboring Rancho El Mirador, and offered me a small adobe home there as a refuge. She had permanent guests, Teddy and Ginny Hayes, living on her ranch. Teddy Hayes, up in his nineties, had been Jack Dempsey's trainer and manager, and was a courtly and gracious friend who always had a kind word for me. Ginny had been a Zeigfeld Follies star. For months, I feasted on their stories.

These people kindly included me in their social life, and that buoyed me. But the crisis that was deadening my life continued to steal purpose and happiness from me, and I was wrestling day by hot day with despair. A second year passed and I was certain I could never find editorial employment again. And I could not forever live on the charity of those who put a roof over my head. I could not bring myself to leave, and I lacked the funds to do so. I had not met an eligible woman or had a date for years, and that, too, only deepened my despair. During the Sasabe years I had turned forty. That was the midpoint. And I had nothing except the knowledge, that would rise in the night, that I lacked inner resilience to battle my way out of trouble.

It was then, as the spring heat built, that I made a fateful decision. I would write a novel. It was a desperate choice. I had not ever imagined that I would be a novelist, and I considered it a fast way to go broke. In fact, I thought it was nuts. But a novel might earn me an exit visa, might put me back in the world.

For years I had been reading western fiction, and one author in particular came to mind, now that I was ensconced in a remote ranch on the border. Gordon Shirreffs, of California, had written all sorts of romantic and engaging western stories set in Arizona and New Mexico, or sometimes in Sonora or Chihuahua, stories brimming with adventure, romance, danger and beautiful Hispanic women. I wondered whether I could write one of those during the off season. Writing a whole book seemed like a formidable project. I had never even written a short story. I had never written dialogue, or fashioned a plot, or attempted to create a character. But I had indeed read several of Shirreffs's novels that were set in the very area where I now lived, and maybe I could garner something from them. And from other western novelists.

I had no idea how to sell the thing even if I succeeded, and no idea what the publishers of western fiction were looking for. But the fear of starvation is a powerful motivator, and I soon began a kamikaze assault on novel-writing, my first draft in longhand on a legal pad. Later I would undertake the ordeal of typing it all up on my Royal portable. I had, all that while, been absorbing life along the border, coming to know and enjoy the many Mexican people there, learning the legends, the myths, the history of that remote country. I had come to love the desert and its unique vegetation. There were stories, hundreds of stories. There were crises, desert thunderstorms that washed out roads and trapped us for days. There was the ongoing drama of the Border Patrol and drug enforcement agents dealing with smugglers, the green Border Patrol vehicles, the buzzing aircraft, and the occasional unlit smuggler plane drifting north at night, bringing contraband up the Altar Valley, hidden by mountains from the national defense radar at Luke Air Force Base.

There were those lovely desert nights, when the heavens glittered with stars in air considered less polluted than anywhere else in the country. Even in summer heat, the soft pleasantness of the air at twilight made for companionship, for a margarita or gin and tonic, or a round of new stories.

I did not know how to write fiction. I did not know how to plot or how to develop a character. I didn't know a thing about dialogue. I sensed that I would have to unlearn everything I had ever learned in journalism and in nonfiction editing, and that proved to be correct. I had a few pocketbooks lying around, my only mentors. They made it look easy. Just invent some character and get him into trouble, and don't worry about literary niceties. Hell, anyone could write a western. Even some guy from the urban upper Middle West who had grown up with *The New Yorker*, not with a livestock journal.

And after all, I had lived as a soi disant horseman up in Montana. I knew a few things. It wasn't as if I didn't know some large and romantic chunks of the American West. So, armed with a legal pad and wavering courage, I began to scribble. That was long before computers were available for word processing. The feel of a ballpoint in my hand was comfortable. I made myself write. I scribbled and stared out the window upon the anonymous desert. I felt the heat build and a managed a chapter or two. I didn't know what I was doing, but at least I had achieved some motion in my becalmed life. On a trip to Tucson I stocked up on typewriter ribbons and carbons and paper, and began banging away on my electric portable. I got frustrated, pitched out pages, redid chapters, all the while certain I would never become a novelist, even a western novelist, which everyone understood to be the lowest species of writer. The stuff was a joke, wasn't it? Just let the hero and villain shoot it out, and that would resolve the story. But even that eluded me.

I suppose it was do or die. That may overdramatize it, but I sensed it had come to that. There was a darkness in me, brooding, ready to overwhelm me, lurking just beyond the sunlit days, a darkness that crept up in the night when I saw myself as some sort of ruined and futureless man. Maybe that was how my life was meant to be.

But then something happened that to this day I regard as the most fateful hinge of my life. It was simple enough. I answered a knock on my door one summer's day to find a trim stranger, cheery, middle-aged, blue-eyed, wearing a battered straw hat and faded ranch clothing.

"I'm Otis Carney, and I live up the road a way. I heard there's a writer living here, and I thought I'd find out about it. I'm a writer myself."

I invited him in. I knew who he was. I knew by reputation

most of the people who lived in that remote world. Otis Carney was a successful novelist and screenwriter and the creator and writer of a television series, The Monroes. He and his wife, Frederika, lived up the road a dozen miles at a place called Las Delicias, another early and historic ranch in the Altar Valley.

I liked this man. He had joy in his eyes and a lively curiosity about his neighbors, even one so obscure that it took effort to track me down. Someone had told him there was a guy in Sasabe, name unknown, who was a writer of some sort. I told him something of my writing life, more or less ashamed at how barren it had become. I told him I was working on a western novel. He had grown up on Chicago's north shore, not far from where I had grown up in Wisconsin. He was several years older, a Marine Corps veteran of World War Two. He had written a best-selling novel, *When the Bough Breaks,* and other books, written many episodes of Dragnet, was a successful television and screen writer, but then he and his wife had decamped from Hollywood, first for a remote ranch in Wyoming that was glorious in the summer but snowbound and isolated winters, and then they had added Las Delicias, for their winters.

At dinner at Las Delicias, I met his wife, Teddy, and later I met their son Peter and his wife Rita, who were operating the ranches. The Carneys had abandoned Beverly Hills for a life in the West, in part to renew themselves. I remember the joy I felt when I discovered that these people loved the worlds of literature and art, politics, ideas, spiritual development, as well as the lore of ranching and life in the Southwest. That was an enchanted evening. The conversation ranged broadly and I drove away some while later not only rejoicing in new friends, but feeling reconnected. One of the gifts Otis gave me was an offer to read my manuscript, what portion of it I felt ready to show him. My novel, dealing with events in that very area of Arizona, had been slowly evolving for several months.

I took him up on it and gave him several chapters. Some

days later, he settled with me on his porch after another dinner, and tackled the story. The news, I soon learned, was not good. Otis lit his pipe, perhaps choosing ways to say things kindly, and then began what might have been a short course in the art of writing fiction.

"We'd better start with your hero," he said. "The problem is, there's nothing wrong with him. He's perfect. Flawless, Stainless. Strong and manly. He says the right things. He does the right things. He thinks the right things. He's not human. Real people have flaws, weaknesses, demons they're wrestling with. Real people are vulnerable, sometimes foolish, miserable on occasion. . . ."

There, in a nutshell, was much of what had gone wrong. Not only was my hero flawless, but also dull. Perfect people are perfectly boring. I had created the dullest superman ever to walk through a story.

We talked about a lot of things: story tension, dialogue, moving from scene to scene without accounting for every moment in a character's life. It was an education, quietly rendered in an enclosed porch of a lovely old adobe ranch house by a man who didn't know me well. Our friendship was only weeks old and yet he had made the effort to analyze a story manuscript and supply me not with just one or two remedies, but a whole kit of them.

And then he handed the story back to me. That particular heap of pages would go into the trash can. But the lessons Otis had given me that evening survived and became a part of my mental equipment, part of the discipline which I have brought to fiction ever since.

The education continued countless other times, not through story analysis, but simply in the ways that Otis and Teddy shared their lives and experiences with me. I set to work on a new version, still ran into trouble, but had the tools now to examine my daily writing and see what might be done. I was still writing longhand on legal pads, and it would be many years before

I began actual composing of a novel on a typewriter, and many more before I turned to computers.

The Carneys had changed my life. I had nothing to give them in return except thanksgiving, and occasional companionship at one or another event or gathering or party or dinner in that remote corner of Arizona. Otis had written his own memoir, mostly about leaving the busy life in Los Angeles to pioneer at a remote ranch on the upper Green River in a wild corner of Wyoming. Random House published his memoir, *New Lease on Life*. Later, when I became a book editor once again, I edited his second memoir, dealing largely with their Arizona sojourn, *The Fence Jumper*, published by Caroline House.

For years afterward, long after I finally left the Sonoran desert, the Carneys shepherded me in my various pursuits. At one point, when I was headed for Los Angeles and what I hoped would be a new life as a screenwriter, they provided valuable contacts and made sure I was welcomed among their many friends there. Otis died early in 2006, and I grieve his loss, and think often of the two people who handed me the keys.

That first novel, *Beneath the Blue Mountain*, was in such a muddle that I finally set it aside. Along the way, I learned that writing fiction was much harder that it seemed; that those guys who made it look easy were actually gifted writers. It wasn't easy at all, and day by day, my respect for those western novelists grew. Somewhat discouraged by my initial effort, I started another one, this time set in Montana in the very country north of Billings where I had bought some acres and raised horses. I made my hero a morose loner with all sorts of vulnerabilities. I was drawing heavily on myself, and also employing the history and terrain that I knew so well when I was a newsman for the *Gazette* in Billings.

After a lot of struggle, I finished the novel and called it *Bushwack*. Little did I realize I had misspelled the word, nor could I imagine that it would eventually be published with a misspelled title. I discovered that my former employer in Illinois, Jameson Campaigne, had started a small publishing company of his own called Caroline House. He was heading for New York on publishing business and volunteered to drop my manuscript off at Doubleday, which had a western library line edited by Jim Menick. Campaigne had a chat with him and left the manuscript. I began the long wait, so familiar to all authors. I turned to the other novel, managed to wrestle it into something I thought was publishable, and started on a third, also set in the Southwest. Then word came: Menick had bought *Bushwack* for a thousand dollars. Campaigne had come through for me, and ever since, I have been grateful to him. It was the beginning of a new life for me, though I didn't know it then.

A contract arrived. I signed it and eventually got the badly needed grand. There was no way I could make a living selling fiction at that price. *Bushwack* had cost me half a year of brutal work as it evolved from a handwritten first draft to a typed second draft to a heavily revised and typed third draft. Still, I rejoiced. I had sold some fiction. Eventually Menick bought my other novel, *Beneath the Blue Mountain*, for fifteen hundred. Two novels. I might be able to make a living at that. Didn't some of those guys churn out a novel every two or three months? Didn't L'Amour write four a year? I tackled a third, this one with a feverish southwestern romance in it, and Menick shot it back to me. It didn't fit his line. It no doubt had too much sex in it, even if there was nothing explicit. There was heavy breathing here and there. So much for anything nontraditional. With that, my career as a fledgling novelist crashed and burned.

3

Los Angeles

I WAS STILL BROKE, STILL ISOLATED, STILL WONDERING WHERE MY NEXT DIME WAS COMING FROM. And my neighbors the Carneys were still offering friendship and were still sharing what they knew of the writing life and art and literature and the West with me. I had spent, in all, about four years on the Arizona border, and plainly it was time to leave. The oil recession was long gone. Publishing was flourishing. Editorial jobs were available. I now had at least a rudimentary knowledge of fiction, and knew something about editing it as well as nonfiction. Yet there was one more detour. I had become so entranced with Otis Carney's anecdotes about Hollywood, and writing for film and television, that I proposed to give it a try. I headed west in my rattletrap pickup truck, rented an apartment in some obscure San Fernando Valley sprawl with a name I can't remember, and began looking for work, any sort of writing work, in the entertainment business. I was no more qualified at that than I was as a novelist, but I was never without certain conceits about my ability.

That was not my first assault on Hollywood. In the mid-1950s I had enrolled in the Pasadena Playhouse as a play writing major. It turned out I was the only one; the rest were acting students. So there I was, learning how to be an actor. Eventually I drifted to Sunset Boulevard, rented a room in a house built by Douglas Fairbanks and Mary Pickford, hung out at Schwab's drugstore, and enrolled in an acting class run by Batami and Benno Schneider. They were refugees from Stalin's purges, and he was the drama coach at Columbia Studio. They had studied under Konstantin Stanislavski, taught Method acting and were somehow associated with Lee Strasberg. One of their students, Bob Francis, had starred in *The Caine Mutiny* only to die in an airplane crash. Another was Kim Novak, who was being coached for her role in *Picnic* when I was there. After the acting class, we always repaired to the Villa Capri, well-hidden from Hollywood Boulevard but actually only a couple of blocks away. It was a famous hangout for Italian singers and movie people. One of its steady customers was James Dean, who was accompanied by his girlfriend Vampira, who was then a local TV personality. She reminded me of someone out of a Charles Addams cartoon. One day, Dean was no longer around, and we discovered he was playing Jett Rink in *Giant*. Then we learned he was dead, having piled up his Porsche north of Los Angeles.

I made friends along the Sunset Strip, worked in a record store to pay some of the freight, set myself up as a glamour photographer (using a rented darkroom) to earn more coin, and somehow survived. One of my photography clients was Kathleen Gallant Weatherby, a model and runner-up Miss America. She was a sweetheart, full of infectious joy, and I was crazy about her. She was dating Frank Sinatra at the time and had a film career going. But she was camera-shy and didn't make it. Last I knew, she had married and divorced Dwight Stuart, of the Carnation Milk Company.

I didn't last long in Hollywood and acting was not my forte. On stage, I walked like a constipated goose and couldn't remember my lines. I decided to get an education while I could, and headed for Madison.

Now, in the late seventies, I was back. The Carneys opened doors for me; a phone call here and there, and at least I was meeting people who counted. I even attended one Beverly Hills A-List party, parking my old truck amid the Mercedes and Bentleys. The hostess, a friend of the Carneys, kindly introduced me to those familiar faces at her soiree and I stuttered through various conversations, and have no recollection of what I said or whether it was coherent. I was surrounded by maybe fifty major movie stars. I wish I could say I enjoyed it; all I can say was that I didn't faint dead away, and did have a long and valuable talk with a screenwriter.

My diligence brought me some work, or so I imagined. At the Sunset Boulevard offices of some obscure production company with a name like "Global International Productions," the porky producer waved me into his modest office. He was on the phone, talking with his wife.

"Gotta go now. My old pal Dick Wheeler's here," he told her, and hung up.

I had never met this man.

"Dick, baby, how are ya?" he said, circling his desk for a handshake. I had never in my life been called Dick baby. I had thought that such things existed only in cartoons. I had not quite believed my ears. Old pal Dick baby. Whatever else might happen to me there on the West Coast, that would make my adventure memorable.

That was our first meeting. What he wanted from me was a treatment, which is a scene-by-scene present-tense description of the story, with maybe some illustrative dialogue thrown in to make a point. He was going to do a film a little like *Jaws*, but instead of a sinister shark, there would be a giant alligator, two stories high and sixty feet long. This would take place in Louisiana. He wanted a redneck hero named Bubba. There would be alligator music, like *Jaws* music, and the monster would rise out of the swamps and gobble little girls on tricycles. There was no way to fight the alligator; his hide was so thick it was like armor.

Inspired, I headed back to my anonymous Valley studio apartment and set to work. I let my imagine loose, and came up with some great scenes. The only way to fight the monster was to flip him over and then shoot him in his soft underbelly, so I envisioned an assault on the beast with forklift trucks. But his lashing tail sends the forklifts flying, and the alligator continues his triumphant rampage. Meanwhile, I had conceived of a perfect Bubba, cunning and strong, with hairy armpits and nostrils. I would pit Bubba against the alligator in scene after scene. When I had finished my treatment, I hied myself to the Sunset Boulevard offices of Global International, or whatever it was, and delivered my opus.

"Dick baby, fine, fine, I'll get back to you," the great man said.

That's when I got my most important lesson about Hollywood. I never heard from him again. I was no longer Dick baby. I was nobody. The whole episode became one of my favorite stories, and many years later there was a surprise response.

"Oh, I saw that film," someone said.

"With Bubba and an alligator and alligator music like *Jaws*, and forklift trucks?"

"Yeah, I'm sure I saw it."

I don't really know whether my idea was stolen by a producer who called me Dick baby, but I never let the truth get in the way of a good story. Over the years, I got a lot of mileage out of that story.

Then I had a break. One day the phone rang:

"This is Susan Oliver," the lady said. "I read your ad in the *Hollywood Reporter*. I'm looking for someone to ghostwrite my story."

I replied that I might be just the person to write it.

I agreed to meet her at her home high in Laurel Canyon, and immediately set to work finding out what I could about her. Susan was by reputation a gorgeous blonde actress with a long and successful career. She had been in *Butterfield 8* with Elizabeth Taylor. She had played Hank Williams' wife Audrey in *Your Cheatin' Heart*. She had starred for years in a soap, *Days of Our Lives*. A 1957 film, *The Green-Eyed Blonde*, had launched her. *Peyton Place* in 1960 had catapulted her to prominence. In between she had played scores of roles in TV westerns. She had credits with Kraft Television Theatre, Armstrong Circle Theater, Playhouse 90, Route 66, and all sorts of other episodes and shows.

Her large Spanish-style home was hidden in a virtual eucalyptus forest, but was close to the road. She let me in, as curious about me as I was about her. She was more petite than I had supposed, but those remarkable cheekbones, that gave her face its character, were her glory, along with that mane of blond hair. She needed no artifice to enhance her beauty. It turned out that she didn't have a film memoir in mind, but something entirely different. She was a pilot. Her heroine was Jackie Cochran. In 1960 she had won the Powder Puff Derby. And what she really wanted was someone to ghost the story of her solo transatlantic flight in a single-engine airplane. Her intent had been to fly clear to Moscow, but that was in the depths of the Cold War and the Soviets would not let her in. Even so, she did fly the Atlantic alone, following Lindbergh's route for the most part. It was a heroic flight and required consummate mastery of aviation, and the arcane grasp of polar navigation.

She was lovely, precise, disciplined, proud of what she had accomplished, and candid. She didn't know who I was or how well I might handle the work. She didn't want to advance money to an unknown writer, but we would work out something. I would do a few chapters and if she liked my work, we would proceed to a full revenue-sharing agreement. It was a risk, but I was confident we would jointly produce an absorbing story.

During the following weeks I spent a lot of time in Laurel Canyon, just talking. At first I took no notes. I wanted to absorb her, and her astrologer mother, and her ways of looking at the world. She told me movie stories, casting and roles and rejections and triumphs. Loves won, loves lost. She talked about her flight training. She talked about her beloved, Mira Slovak, an air force pilot who had fled Communist Czechoslovakia in a MIG 21 and had become a Cold War hero. That had been the beginning of Susan's lifelong enchantment with Eastern European males. Gradually I switched to note-taking, and recorded the story. She flew the Atlantic in an Aero Commander, the Cadillac of light planes at that time. She had mastered the aircraft, mastered flying in extreme northern latitudes, mastered the difficulties involved in refueling at a tiny airstrip deep in a fog-bound fjord in Greenland.

It was a great story, and the more time I spent with Susan, the more I admired her. Her ambitions, her life, extended far beyond Hollywood. My interviews occurred at all hours, whenever she could slide me into her busy schedule. We talked during meals, while we were driving somewhere, mornings and evenings. I wanted a deeper sense of her character, the things that had driven her to this flight. I focused on her ambitions, her passions, and the occasional darknesses and sorrows of an oddly lonely life. She was a member of the Academy of Motion Picture Arts and Sciences, and was in the process of becoming a director, forever spreading her wings.

Then I started in on my typewriter, opening the story at the very moment that she took off in a New Jersey rainstorm, retracted the wheels, and headed into the unknown. She did not even know whether she would receive permission to continue to Moscow. Everything ahead was a mystery and a risk. But the first task was to cross the Atlantic, and then see what awaited her. I had to put myself in her head, catch her train of thought, feel what she felt as her wheels lifted off the wet tarmac and she sailed into a rainy overcast over the Atlantic. I finished fifty pages or so, proud of what I had written. The story began with liftoff, and then cut back to the impossible dream, and the long process of fulfilling it.

It was time to show her the work. I dropped it off and she accepted it with smiles. Then I waited. A day or two passed. Plainly, she had not sat down and plunged right in, but that was understandable. Then one afternoon the phone rang.

"I hate it!" she yelled. "I just hate it. It's not me! It has nothing to do with me!"

She was howling so loudly that I had to hold the receiver several inches from my ear, and even then the howling was all I could stand. I simply listened, desolately. She finally wound down, and that was the end of it, I thought. I could not maintain myself in costly Southern California any more. I hung up, stared at the bleak little studio apartment in some nameless burg in the Valley, and knew the jig was up. But there was a tender ending, after all. She called later, apologized, offered me two hundred bucks. We agreed to have a dinner together before I left town. I took her in my rattling pickup to a Mexican place, where we soon were mobbed by fans. She graciously signed napkins, menus, slips of paper. Mostly these people recognized her from *Days of Our Lives*. They kept asking me for my autograph, and I told them I was nobody. And still they insisted, so I signed a few, and they studied my name with a blank look. Blank looks can be a mercy. To this day I can eat anywhere and suffer no recognition. For a while Susan and I corresponded, and then the notes stopped, and later I learned she had died in 1990 of cancer. I sorrowed. It was only after her death that I heard that Susan did eventually write her own memoir of the flight, but I have been unable to find it.

4

Heading East

BROKE AS USUAL. The only thing I had gotten out of Los Angeles was the surety that I needed to acquire some business sense. And a new vocation. I was adrift again. I don't remember how events fell out after that, or in what order, but it isn't important. I landed an editing job, this time with Icarus Press in South Bend. It had been founded by Bruce Fingerhut, a colleague of mine at Open Court. Icarus had found a ready market for its product, which was coffee-table sports books focusing on Notre Dame. I knew nothing about Notre Dame except that football was a passion there. But it was pleasant work. I edited sports copy, wrote elaborate cutlines for the illustrated books, and settled in. There was an appetite for coffee table books featuring Notre Dame, and Fingerhut's little company was feeding it. The university campus was handsome and traditional, but South Bend was not exactly a place to make my own. From the day I arrived to the day I left, I starved for the West. It was a salary, it was security, it was easy work that I did well: what more could I ask? Here again, I heard the stories. Old John Grant, who had been on the Notre Dame team with the Four Horsemen, wandered in and out to entertain us with his endless supply of anecdotes and sports lore.

Then one spring, as restless as the geese honking their way north, I abandoned South Bend. I didn't have a job but I had a little cash in my pockets, and Montana was calling me. I rented an apartment in Helena, wrote a contemporary novel called *Paradise Valley* that never sold, worked for a while with the Montana Press Association editing its newsletter, and set to work on a western that would deal with the terrible winter of 1886 and 1887, which killed most of the range cattle in Montana and forever changed the nature of ranching in the West. I set it on what today is one of Montana's great ranches, the N-Bar, near Grass Range. It was country I knew and loved, and prowled once again for my novel. And oh, it was heaven to escape the Midwest.

A story took shape. The hero, Quin Putnam, would be anything but the usual western down-at-the-heels cowboy. I made him a Bostonian and a Harvard man who had come west, perhaps a bit like Owen Wister. I took care to heed Otis Carney's advice, and kept my hero human and vulnerable. Even there, a thousand miles from my mentor, his counsel was guiding me. Putnam's adversaries were some Britons, powerful and sometimes eccentric and usually wise. That was historically accurate. The ranching West was largely developed with English capital and expertise, and today cattle such as Herefords and Angus from the British Isles populate modern ranches. The issue in my novel was fencing the open range, but Quin's struggles to claim and fence pasture are trumped by the terrible winter of 1886, and the die-off of most of the Territory's cattle. I thought it was a good novel, but I had no entre to New York publishing at that time.

I was reaching out during that period, looking for serious freelance work, and I found it. The widow of Major General Charles H. Corlett, of Espanola, NM, was looking for an editor who could take her husband's extensive memoir of World War Two, polish and edit it, and find a publisher for it. She was willing to share the proceeds of any sale but there would be no payment up front. I took on the task, though it soon became obvious that the project was doomed. General Corlett's memoir was thin, and he was no longer around to help me flesh it out. He had a long Army career, and at the time of D-Day and the Normandy invasion he was the commanding officer of the XIX Corps, and a major figure in General Eisenhower's army. But his command had faltered in the grueling struggle around Saint-Lo, and eventually he was relieved. He wanted to defend his career record, and wrote his memoir. There were all sorts of names flying off the typed pages, but these officers needed to be fleshed out, given personalities, explained. Without the general, I was on my own, and other World War Two memoirs and histories weren't much help. All I could do, at bottom, was edit it and supply a few facts drawn from other sources.

I sent it to an old-line New York literary agency, and it was respectfully received and read at once. But the result was predictable. Without a major fleshing out, the memoir could not be published. I sent the bad news back to the widow and received a polite thank you. I had invested a lot of effort for nothing, once again. Over the years I had walked into several such arrangements, sometimes to my sorrow. Later the family retrieved my rights to a share of the proceeds, and I suspect the memoir was privately published, though I have been unable to locate a copy. That was the last time I offered to do editorial work without some sort of advance payment. I have little business sense, and I was slow to grasp that many people think that writing is something that requires neither significant labor nor skill, and thus deserves little or no pay. I had learned an important lesson.

I was going broke in Helena but not for the lack of trying. I wrote another contemporary novel, grounded on a swift, bittersweet romance there. I was heading for middle age; there was a beautiful, bright and lovely young lady of twenty-seven in the apartment above. It didn't last long. Soon she was back with someone her own age, and I was alone again. I turned the affair into a novel which was never published.

No money, not much prospect for work in Montana. No future in the West. No significant publishers, no magazines that might pay something. And yet I was so deeply rooted in the open and rural West that I couldn't bear to leave. Wasn't there a writers organization that dealt with western fiction? Maybe some contacts would western writers would be helpful. Whatever the name of the group was, it was well hidden. It didn't advertise itself. But I hunted for it, and finally found a list of genre fiction societies in a *Writers Market* at the Lewis and Clark library. It was called Western Writers of America; its secretary-treasurer was a man named Rex Bundy, and he lived over in the Bitterroot Valley south of Missoula. I wrote him. He sent me an application.

I discovered at once that WWA was a thoroughly professional group, and there were membership barriers. I didn't qualify for active membership but my two Doubleday westerns plus other things could slide me in as an associate. There would be a convention in Santa Fe in June. Maybe I should go. Maybe meet some western authors. There might even be an editor or two present, or an agent or two. I had nothing to lose except more money. I couldn't afford a trip to costly Santa Fe, but sometimes you have to take chances.

Meanwhile I was curious about Bundy, and arranged to drive to his home near Victor, Montana, for a visit. I piled into my venerable truck and headed west, wondering what the hell I was doing. But I found the house, and Rex and his wife greeted me effusively and talked me into staying for dinner. I discovered something then and there: writers of the American West love to get together and are the most affable and affectionate people on earth. I was the humblest addition to their membership, with a couple of library hardcovers that never earned a nickel beyond their tiny advances, had received no reviews, and had generated no correspondence. But that didn't matter. By the time I left for home, I had a good idea what the convention would be like. There would be perhaps a hundred fifty people, including some of the grandest names in the field. My idol, Gordon Sherriffs would probably be present. Yes, there would be chances to meet them all; meet editors and agents.

The convention would be at the Inn at Loretto, the lovely southwestern-style hostelry just off the plaza. I opted to stay at the cheaper of the accommodations offered to members, the Posada de Santa Fe on Palace Street, a few blocks away. I wouldn't know a soul. Bundy had a heart condition and wasn't going. I am reserved, if not shy, and I suspected that I would arrive as a stranger and leave as a stranger. And yet I went.

I have always loved Santa Fe, as much because it is a feast for the senses as for its history, its unique Hispanic culture, its lovely setting in the foothills of the Sangre de Cristos, and for its cultural ambience. It had generated its own art and literature. Now, in Santa Fe, I was attending my first western writers convention and loving it. La Posada was a marvel, with adobe casas spread over a wide ground. The Inn at Loretto, elegantly melding with older structures in the area, was a perfect place for a writers group to gather.

I thought I would know not a soul, but I was wrong. At the opening reception I encountered Jeanne Williams, whom I had met in Sasabe at the home of her brother, the postmaster. Petite and dark and beautiful and always clad elegantly, Jeanne welcomed me with great warmth and promptly introduced me to everyone in sight. She was the author of many novels of the West, the winner of several Spur Awards and the Levi Strauss Saddleman award for lifetime contributions to western literature, and there she was, shepherding me through my first convention.

I was among people I enjoyed, who were welcoming me, asking about my work and life. It was a good beginning. I discovered I was among some great talents. WWA had been formed in 1953 by various western novelists, who invited the pulp short story writers to join them in a traditional authors guild, expressly modeled on Mystery Writers of America, which had been founded a few years earlier. The new guild would look after the interests of members, promote the literature of the American West, improve relationships with publishers, give Spur Awards to the outstanding literature published each year, and hold annual conventions where editors, agents and authors could get together, do business, exchange opinions, and air problems.

I attended the book signing, which was in an ancient courtyard on Palace Street, and bought a mystery by an obscure novelist whose name was Tony Hillerman. He was there, signing his novels, and he signed my first edition copy of *The Dark Wind* this way: "For Richard Wheeler—please note the importance of thinking about vandalized windmills while plotting. Tony Hillerman." It now resides in a Mylar jacket in my bookcase. Last I knew, it was worth about seven hundred bucks.

I had read enough western fiction to know I was in good company. But at that convention I mostly kept to myself. I wanted to watch and listen. Quite by accident, I sold my *Winter Grass* novel. I had noticed that there was a display of western hardcover books published by Walker and Company, a publisher I was not familiar with. These were typical library-line western stories, competing with Doubleday's DD western line. Its editor, Sara Ann Freed, was on hand.

The patio at the Loretto was a popular gathering place, where many of these authors and editors gathered for iced tea or something stronger in the mild sun. (I was to learn, over the years, that WWA is a hard-drinking outfit.) I asked whether I might join one of the tables, and was welcomed. Two of those at that table turned out to be Sara Ann Freed, and her husband Ira Weissman. It was a pleasant social afternoon. Later, after I returned to Helena and she to New York, I wrote her at Walker and asked whether she would look at a novel I had written, and reminded her that we had met at Santa Fe. She agreed to have a look. I shipped off *Winter Grass* and began that long wait that is well known by most authors. Then she wrote back saying yes, she wanted it, with a few revisions, and this: "You're a real writer!"

She would buy it for three grand. I could scarcely process my good fortune. Instead of turn-downs, here was an acceptance. The revision notes turned out to be something I could easily deal with, and in due course I got a contract and half an advance. Fifteen hundred bucks didn't bail me out of my chronic poverty but it was some of the most welcome cash ever to drift my way, and I was feeling pretty bright-eyed. I knew that attending WWA conventions and being an active part of a western writers organization were crucial to a western writing career. I was witnessing the reality, the essence, of what a professional writers guild could offer its members. On countless occasions since then, I've advised people who are eager to break into the field to attend the genre fiction convention of their choice. As for me, the membership dues I hesitantly paid out that first time, were returned to me a hundredfold.

But Santa Fe proved to have other, darker facets. Unbeknownst to me in my isolation from fellow novelists over the years, western fiction was under siege. That was the tumultuous period in American letters, where most of our literature was being reexamined. Western novels had gradually become the central American myth, an explanation of who we are, how we expanded, and what our character had become. With westerns we explained ourselves to the world. But there in Santa Fe, one peaceful afternoon when the panels were humming along, my world was abruptly challenged. At first it was simply the droning of a cynical academic, saying that cowboys were merely agricultural laborers and authors had romanticized them. In essence, the scholar was denying that cowboys had romanticized themselves or their lore, and had never so much as sung a ballad to their lives.

Well, all right. We were living in a debunker's paradise.

But then a group of locals barged in, commandeered the podium and mike, and began denouncing us. We were, they said, celebrating cultural genocide. We were racists. We were celebrating the triumph of white men over Indians. We were, in essence, fascists and authoritarians. We were imposing our values on people who didn't want or accept them. It was quite an indictment, shouted at us as we involuntarily froze in our seats. And any objections from the audience, such as that a lot of western fiction was exactly the opposite of what they had claimed it to be, got shouted down. After an interminable time, the perpetrators of this little cultural mission marched out, angry and looking offended to be in our very presence.

There was some truth in the accusations. But I also knew of novels and films that celebrated these people and defended their ways. I had caught my first glimpse of a subterranean conflict that would continue to the present, erupting now and then in new accusations and defenses. Western literature was and is under siege.

At the Spur Banquet that evening I sat beside Damaris Rowland, who was then Berkley's western editor, and William Kittredge, who was writing a western series along with Stephen Krauzer under the pseudonym of Owen Rountree. These were far from traditional westerns, featuring hip heros and heroines, people with contemporary social values even though they remained in 19th century circumstances. Sometimes they were inadvertently funny, especially to someone familiar with the actual values of people who lived in the latter part of the 19th century. But I greatly enjoyed sharing a table with Kittredge, an amiable bear of a man, and a Missoula, Montana, English professor.

I headed north through the back-country West, avoiding Interstates as much as possible. I've absorbed much of the

American west simply by sticking to its rural roads and blotting up the scenery, the ranches and river valleys and clouded peaks.

5

Midwestern Editor

IWOULD HAVE TO ABANDON HELENA. My stab at free-lancing had failed. And now, at last, an editing job had opened up for me. My erstwhile employer at Open Court Publishing Company, Jameson Campaigne, had started his own publishing company in Ottawa, another small town on the Illinois River. Would I care to return to Illinois as a book editor? Editing serious economics and public affairs books would be a joy, no matter that the work would be done surrounded by pancake-flat cornfields. But leaving the West to go where the work might be found was a heavy decision for me, especially with some promise of a career writing western fiction. I still had to earn my bread, and an occasional advance for a western novel wasn't going to do the job. I drove east, my truck full of my honed-down possessions.

I rented a small house in Ottawa and reported for

work in a downtown second-floor office. Most of the time my sole companion there was a secretary-receptionist. Campaigne was a night owl and rarely showed up until four or five, working steadily to one or two in the morning. So I rarely saw him, and the disparity of our hours sometimes made editing difficult. We communicated with notes and memos and post-it stickers. Still, I had a good job, working among affectionate people, and I had much to be delighted about. The Campaignes treated me very kindly. And Ottawa wasn't so bad, really. Life along the Illinois River was lively.

Campaigne was a libertarian public affairs wonk, but he also had a fascination for the fur trade and mountain men, and that had led to a discovery. He had been in touch with an unknown writer named Terry Johnston who had penned a massive novel of the fur trade, with a trapper named Scratch as its hero. The book was enormous, badly written, lacking grammar—and magical. So powerful was Johnston's story of wilderness life, dangers at every hand, fur-trade lore and adventure, that the story triumphed over all of the inadequacies in the storytelling. Campaigne had gone ahead with the project, knowing it would be huge and costly but he believed that something marvelous could be wrought from Terry Johnston's novel if it could be edited down and disciplined. So he had contracted to publish it. Terry finally acquired a publisher after years of struggle and rejection. All this had happened long before I arrived at Caroline House Publishers. Campaigne had found an excellent editor, Bill Decker, Spur Award-winning novelist and an editor at an Ohio University Press, and put Decker to work on the story. It was a massive task, and it took a long time for Decker to put the giant novel into some sort of shape. Then Campaigne had shipped it to Johnston for approval. The novel came back with virtually all the editing rejected, save only for some corrected spelling.

There was a lot of back-and-forth, I learned, but in the end, *Carry the Wind* had been published almost entirely as

Johnston wrote it. The author had rigidly rejected virtually all alteration. Even so, thanks to a striking jacket and good flap copy, the book succeeded, and found its way into a whole fraternity of buckskinners and black-powder shooters, who had been starved for mountain-man fiction and had seen precious little of it since A. B. Guthrie, Jr, had penned *The Big Sky*.

Now, upon my arrival, Terry was finishing up his second novel, a sequel called *Border Lords*. And I was to edit it. I began by reading the first, wincing my way past the clumsy stuff, but admiring the breathtaking grandeur of it. Johnston was some sort of genius, no matter that portions of the story were barbarous. I didn't know how much luck I might have, but I plunged into the editing, trimming overwrought passages, imposing some sort of discipline on the narrative. I decided simply to tell him exactly what I was doing and why; I had no magical means to slide my editing past him, but at least I could explain my decisions in notes.

I soon encountered a major problem. He had begun this second novel in the series without reintroducing his protagonists. His main characters were simply names, without history, without even physical descriptions. Terry had apparently assumed that readers of *Borderlords* would have read *Carry the Wind*, and would know his characters. I wrote him, explaining that each book in a series must stand on its own. One cannot assume that the buyer of the second book has read the earlier one and knows who these characters are. The solution was straightforward and simple. He needed to rework the first chapters, sliding in descriptions of the characters, so readers of the second book would be able to understand these characters without having read the first. To my astonishment, Terry refused. He would not alter a word, and that was final.

We had a major dilemma. The book was not publishable as it stood. I sent the edited manuscript back to him, only to have my entire editing rejected. I discovered, to my chagrin, that I too had made errors, mostly because of my ignorance of mountain men, their lingo, and the lore of the fur trapping era. He used these as levers to proclaim my incompetence, and the exchanges did nothing to draw us toward common ground. Then Terry pressed the nuclear button. The hell with Caroline House; he was taking his story elsewhere. Campaigne badly wanted to publish the book, but had no ideas about how to proceed.

I had new friends from Western Writers of America, Jory and Charlotte Sherman. He was a veteran novelist along with his wife, and well versed in buckskinning and fur trade lore. He was more diplomatic than I, and might have better luck with Terry. The upshot was that the company hired the Shermans to edit Terry's novel. Jory proceeded with the editing, Charlotte painfully typed the cleaned-up pages, which was an enormous task, and then they invited Terry to their Missouri home to approve of the editorial changes. They succeeded in part, because what Terry saw was the cleaned-up and retyped pages, and didn't see the originals.

But in one area, Terry was adamant. He would not rewrite the opening chapters to reintroduce the characters, so *Borderlords* depended entirely on the previous novel. When the Shermans finally persuaded Terry that it was necessary to make *Borderlords* stand on its own, Terry resolved the matter by introducing long passages from *Carry the Wind*, using italics. The result was bizarre. In the early chapters of *Borderlords* are endless italicized inserts from the previous novel, which made the whole beginning murky and hard to grasp. He had kept his word: nothing would be rewritten. And so the book went to press, and drew sharply negative comment.

That was the beginning of a lifelong, stormy, affectionate, difficult and yet rewarding friendship with Terry. When he lay dying at St. Vincent's Hospital in Billings a few years ago, he had lost his ability to speak, but he took my hand and held it, and in that moment all was forgiven. We would remember only the good things, the endorsements we gave each other, the times we had helped each other. (He had helped me more than I had helped him.) And he forgave me for being an ass, which I had been in my dealings with him. He died a few days later, and I knew I had lost an extraordinary friend and colleague.

I continued to toil at Caroline House, which had changed its name to Green Hill, and later, to Jameson Books. The days edged by slowly because the company was too cash-starved to require a full-time in-house editor. There were plenty of projects, but not enough income to pay for copyediting, proofreading, typesetting, printing, publicity, and promotion. I had little to do. I had worked through the slushpile and was pouncing on all manuscripts as soon as they arrived. With no editing at hand, I turned to promotion and publicity. My primary task was to inform reviewers about our books, and see about getting reviews. This often took the form of a personal letter to reviewers, pointing out what was unique about the book. I also began identifying and writing organizations that might be interested in bulk purchases. I did not neglect librarians, either. I developed press releases targeted to special groups.

The company was publishing all sorts of books, ranging from public affairs to self-help. It even had a book coming out about adult incontinence, a pioneering effort that appeared long before June Allyson was touting absorbent throwaway products on television. But as the months and years passed, I cannot say that my promotional efforts achieved much, nor was the little company prospering. I wondered how long I might be employed. I wondered what else I could do to jack up sales. We did a couple more buckskin-type novels, and had some success selling these off the tailgates of trucks at black-powder meets and rendezvous around the country.

We published Win Blevins, who was evolving into a major novelist of the fur trade. Over the years, Win's novels added richness and grace and elegance to the whole realm of fur trade fiction. We published a nonfiction book by Loren Estleman called *The Wister Trace*, his well-considered examination of the best western fiction from its early days to the present. It required no editing, for which I was grateful, because he is among those authors who reject it. He told me that he always responds politely to editors and then ignores the editing, which he believes only damages his work. Such is his ability that he is probably right, though I am of the view that authors usually profit from a sensitive editing, if only because we all have blind spots, and editors are actually readers' advocates, making authors aware of difficulties.

I was desk-bound and unable to attend the WWA convention in the Amarillo area in 1983, but my employer went, and did his best to sell his various black-powder novels to the assembled western writers. I had become an impassioned advocate and member of WWA, and treasured the friendships I had formed in Santa Fe. But I remained in Ottawa, mostly twiddling my thumbs because there was little to do and no money to put more titles into production. I intended to go to the next western writers convention in Branson, Missouri, in 1984.

One of the virtues of working in central Illinois was that I could visit my family in Wisconsin periodically. Some of my siblings as well as my mother lived in the Milwaukee area. On one of those trips, I received a surprising phone call at my mother's house. It was from Rita. She was at the nearby Holiday Inn. She wanted to see me. I'd had no contact with her for many years, but I knew she had been institutionalized at a sanitarium not far from my mother's home.

When she let me into her motel room, I was chilled. The tall, striking girl I had married long before had become a little gnome I scarcely recognized. She peered at me from eyes that were not hers. She was inhabited by something else, someone beyond my fathoming. She talked in gusts of anger, her train of thought impossible to follow. But one thing was clear: she had escaped the sanitarium and wanted me to pay for her motel bill. I would not do it. I sat there, across from her, thinking that if ever there was a case for demonic possession, I was staring right at it. I felt sick at heart, not because of any residual love, but because

I was seeing the utter ruin of a person I had once held in my arms with joy. It soon ended. I fled. Some days later the hotel manager tried to extract payment from me. She had been there most of a week before he got suspicious. He had gotten my name from her. I turned him down.

I heard nothing from her for another year or so, and then in 1984 there was a call, this time to my home in Illinois. She didn't go through any preliminaries. "I'm dying of lung cancer," she said. "I have a few days left. I'm in a hospital."

While I was absorbing that she enjoyed her last joke. "I asked the doctors if there was anything I could do," she said. "And they said I could quit smoking." It was her last laugh. She died a few weeks later, though the event slipped past me. No one in her family called or wrote. No one in my family noticed. She was forty-four. Sometimes in the middle of a night, I imagine myself walking beside her through the stars. I tell her I loved her and wished it could be different. I tell her I am sorry I failed her. I sense that her spirit is free now of all those darknesses that burdened it, and there is a beautiful and loving Rita somewhere beyond the horizon. Freed from the hell of madness, she is in a better place.

Winter Grass had been published by Walker and Company in 1983, and much to my delight it was a Spur Award finalist. It had even garnered a good review or two. That meant going to Branson. In those days, the winners of the Spur Awards were kept secret; only the finalists were made public before the convention and the award ceremony. So there was a chance I might have an award-winning novel. Sara Ann Freed would be on hand, and between us, we would see what fate might bring.

That June of 1984 I headed for Branson, the Ozarks resort town patronized primarily by Texans wanting to vacation among a few hills and lakes. The convention was to have been held in a new convention center being developed by Janet Daily's husband. But it was never built, and the convention was shoehorned into an inadequate entertainment hotel, essentially a theater with rooms and a cafeteria attached. We could use the theater by day for our meetings, but we could not use it past four because of the musical shows scheduled there. No meeting rooms existed. The only restaurant was a cafeteria with a service island in the middle, and picnic benches for tables. There was no bar, but we were permitted to keep our own booze in a tiny room, along with ice and mixers. We had a grand time, because western authors are happy to collect anywhere, but mostly we went out on the town. And when the Spur Awards rolled around in that cafeteria, after we had slid our plastic trays along the island rail and filled our plates from food bins in the island, Sara Ann and I hunkered at a picnic table and awaited the result. The hit of the evening was a funny talk by Doc Sonnichsen, author of several delightful nonfiction studies of the cranky American southwest. He did not spare the hotel or the convention, but his thrusts were always cheerful.

I remained a finalist. I was beaten by Frank Roderus, whose *Leaving Kansas* won in that category. But I had a fine certificate to hang on my wall, and the knowledge that my third western novel had come very close to being the best of the year. It was great to see Sara Ann. It had been great to renew friendships and meet new people. That disastrous accommodation inspired the WWA board of directors to draw up some standards for future conventions, and Vice President Francis Fugate soon reported to the membership with a clear set of requirements about what accommodations and services a host hotel must have. And the new requirements mandated that there be a local member involved with the convention.

I fled the Ozarks, finding them claustrophobic and somehow sinister, though the very idea that those hills and hollows were hiding nasty things would offend all those godly sorts who have made Branson a sort of Jerusalem. Many years later I sallied one more time into the Ozarks, met some pleasant and delightful people at the annual meeting of an Ozarks writers group, but I was glad to escape back into the West where there was open country and horizons. If land shapes people, then Ozarks people are full of secrets, and what happens in those hollows of the heart and mind rarely sees daylight.

Sara Ann Freed, meanwhile, was pursuing her own career options. She had developed the Walker and Company library line of western fiction, starting with no knowledge at all of the field. She got good advice, read through the classics, and began by reprinting some major western titles and authors, and then feeding new authors into the line. I became one of those, and with the success of *Winter Grass* I was able to get contracts for two more books, which turned out to be *Sam Hook* and *Richard Lamb*. But Sara was gone, and she was replaced by young Michael Sagalyn. But more about him later. Sara Ann moved over to M. Evans and Company, a bright, high-quality publisher of trade fiction and nonfiction, sometimes compared to Farrar, Straus, Giroux. They, too, wanted a library western line, and she was going to create it for them. Later, she moved to Mysterious Press, became one of its top editors, and stayed there. She loved mysteries, and found her niche at last.

But I continued in Illinois, underemployed because of the company's chronic cash crunch. Still, I was treated well, had a secure job, and it seemed likely that I would spin out my life there. Maybe the company would prosper and I would some day actually have things to do. I was pretty much alone. Campaigne wasn't there during normal business hours and was often away for weeks at a stretch. That meant that decisions didn't get made, or I made them at my own risk, subject to his repeal. In 1985 I took a vacation trip to Santa Fe, going via Amtrak, detraining at Lamy, outside of the old pueblo. It fired up all my fevers again. I needed the West; either Montana or New Mexico, the only places where my spirit rejoiced.

In June of 1985 I picked up Win Blevins in St. Louis, where

he was indulging in his favorite pastime, watching his beloved Cardinals play ball. We headed for San Antonio, site of the next WWA convention. It was being held in an old but serviceable hotel there, and it didn't matter that the roof leaked. We were all having a great party, and this time we had a real bar dishing out the drinks. San Antonio had great Tex-Mex restaurants, the River Walk, and the Alamo. We made the best of it. I made lifelong friends there. It had taken a couple of conventions to get past a native shyness, but suddenly these people were all brothers and sisters. That year I got to know nonfiction writer and editor Dale L. Walker, who received a special Spur Award at that time for his five years as editor of *The Roundup* Magazine. He had taken it from a humdrum house organ into a lively, combative, ten-a-year publication that did much to advance the literature of the West. I had contributed a few things to the magazine and now was realizing he was one of the shrewdest, most gifted bookmen in American literature. He was the director of Texas Western University Press at that time. I also got to know Bob Conley, author of several excellent western novels dealing with the Cherokees and their history. He went on to win numerous awards for his writing. I met Don and Eddie Coldsmith, to my everlasting delight. He is a physician turned novelist and was producing absorbing stories about the first contact of Europeans and Indians, mostly from an Indian perspective; she was a special ed teacher, retired now, full of funny anecdotes. I became an acolyte of New Mexico novelist Max Evans. He had penned some comic masterpieces such as *The Rounders* that had been turned into movies or television series. I met feisty Norman Zollinger and Ginna Malone, and came to admire the New Mexico novelist and his lovely psychologist wife.

There was an afterglow following those conventions. It was as if people didn't want to go home, but just wanted to linger there among friends. After the Spur Award ceremony there was a party called the Campfire, where we crowded into a hotel bedroom or suite, there to enjoy one last hurrah, drink beer or soft drinks drawn from ice in the bathtub, and share our final moments together. Dick House, a past president, would recite the poems of Robert Service and various slightly bawdier ones. There would be comic Buffalo Awards bestowed by Lenore Carroll, of Kansas City, on unsuspecting people. Charlie Eckhart would arrive with his noxious cigar, but politely smoke it out on the patio. Cherry Weiner and other agents would arrive, sit on the beds, and watch the antics. But the hour would come when we all filtered to our rooms. That year's party was over. But even then it was not quite over. The next morning, in the dining room, we table-hopped, saying our goodbyes for the year.

Win and I left for the north. Part of the fun of the trip had been traveling with him. He has an advanced degree in musical and literary criticism from Columbia University, and as we talked and argued our way down the highways and byways, I was receiving an education. He had written one of the classics of the literature of the fur trade, *Give Your Heart to the Hawks*, which is still in print and still revered for its pungent explorations of life among the mountain men. We had reprinted his novel about Sacajawea's son, Jean-Baptiste Charbonneau, and had published his tender novel, *Silk and Shakespeare*. Since then, he has gone on to publish numerous richly textured novels as well as the most authoritative and complete encyclopedia of western terms and words.

Times were changing for me. One day I learned that Michael Sagalyn was leaving his position as Walker's western editor and the company was looking for a replacement. I saw my chance and wrote at once: I would like to edit the line from Montana. I was sure I could manage it, in spite of the distances involved. My offer was accepted, and soon my life would change dramatically. I understood I would acquire and edit one western novel a month for Walker, for a thousand dollars a book. It wasn't much but it was a core income I could take west with me. And I was soon to learn that it would mean acquiring only eight a year because of Walker's existing contracts with Lauren Paine. I would really have to scramble to stay afloat. But in October of 1985 I headed west once again, bringing my employment with me. And there would be time to write.

6

Canyon Creek

I SET UP THE WESTERN OFFICE OF WALKER AND COMPANY ATOP THE CONTINENTAL DIVIDE, at Flesher Pass, between Helena and Lincoln, Montana. An A-frame cabin was available from my friend Ingrid Semple, and I rented it for a hundred a month. It was a summer place, so I installed baseboard electric heat and a larger woodstove to winterize it. My nearest neighbors were two mountain women who supported themselves by doing odd jobs, including log home construction and cutting cordwood. My postal address was Canyon Creek, which was twenty miles down the grade toward Helena. All in all, if I didn't get too lonely or isolated, it would be a good place to set up shop. In fact I eventually did get cabin fever, and after two years moved to Big Timber, where I could enjoy some social life.

At first I scarcely noticed the isolation. I hade plenty

to do. My new colleague at Walker and Company, Jacqueline Johnson, began shipping manuscripts to me. I, in turn, was telling my writing friends that I would be buying genre western fiction. The manuscripts began flowing in almost at once. I had very few slots to fill: eight a year minus the two novels that I intended to write. However, my own sales to Walker were not a foregone conclusion. I had to write up proposals and sample chapters, and have my agent submit them to Jackie, who was to treat them like anyone else's work, probing them for marketability and strengths and weaknesses. Two a year was as many as I could manage. I was still writing them on legal pads and then painfully typing them up and revising them. Computers were in their infancy, and few writers were using them.

During my sojourn in Illinois, I had acquired an agent. Ray Puechner, who specialized in genre fiction, especially westerns and mysteries, lived in Milwaukee of all places, and was operating a successful agency from that odd corner of the literary world. On my various trips to Wisconsin to see my family, I had often stopped at Ray's southside house, just to have a cup of coffee with him and talk shop with Ray and his sister Millie. Ray had a remarkable clientele, including Loren Estleman, Ed Gorman, Gary Paulsen, and Joe Lansdale. It didn't seem to matter that he was operating so far from New York; his contacts were as close as the telephone. It was Ray who had brokered the sale of Estleman's nonfiction to Green Hill when I was editing there. Ray talked softly and I had to strain to hear him. His clients accused him of mumbling, but that isn't quite the proper word. He was a whisperer, and it was especially difficult to follow him on the phone, when one had no lips to read. I listened closely because he knew the publishing business better than anyone I had met, and was also the master of all sorts of arcana about pulp fiction. He loved jazz, especially anything with a throaty saxophone, and I often heard music wafting through the telephone system when we talked. He was mostly bald, cheerful, cynical, and had been through assorted hells as an alcoholic. But now he was dry, operating his kitchen-table literary agency, and doing well.

The manuscripts began rolling in from Ray as well as other agents and various unagented authors. Scores of manuscripts. Heaps of manuscripts. Many of them came from friends in Western Writers of America, but also from strangers. These came, as the saying goes, over the transom. Somebody had gotten my name and shipped off his magnum opus. I would read until my eyes blurred, break for a hike along the two-rut road wending through pine forest, and go back to the reading. The bad stories were easy: I had a stack of Walker rejection slips and used them. Bad stories written by friends were tougher. These required a gentle letter, and perhaps a blueprint for revising the story into something I could use. My task was to buy genre western fiction, set in the late 19th century, in the 60,000-word range; stories of a sort that might be reprinted by mass market houses. Walker had publicized those standards, and yet many of the submissions did not even remotely qualify. Too long, too short, too historically early, too late, too this or that. These I would dutifully stuff into their wrappers, hoping the authors had included return postage, and ship them back. Many authors didn't include a return envelop or postage, and I usually had to deal with these out of my own pocket.

I bought some dandy stories written by Gary Paulsen. He was not a western writer, nor was he a member of any writers organization. Even then he was establishing himself as the premier writer of young adult novels in the country, and had won the Newbery Prize. He lives now outside of White Oaks, New Mexico, figuratively at the end of the road, and has written about 175 novels. His stories were so good I would gladly take whatever I could get from him; after I left, Jackie Johnson continued to buy his westerns. Along the way, Paulsen gave me excellent advice about sales, agents, writing genre fiction, and he always offered encouragement as well. He awakened in me the understanding that good western literature need not come from "western writers."

Editors and authors see the world of acquisitions very differently. Editors receive tons of submissions, many of them perfectly publishable, and yet editors are constantly looking for the magical story, the one that distinguishes itself from its competition. I could have bought acceptable stories right and left; but I wanted to buy memorable ones. Authors rightly wonder why their perfectly serviceable stories are returned. It is simply because there are hundreds, maybe thousands, of other marketable stories. Once in a while I hurt people. Old friends, expecting me to buy their stories, were sometimes shocked when I returned them. One in particular replied tartly and cold-shouldered me for a couple of years after I had turned down three of his novels. But the stark reality was that he didn't quite grasp how to write compelling fiction, and his characters were wooden too. I was embarrassed, and went to Jackie Johnson for support. Would she read those submissions and confirm or reject my verdicts? She would, and she concurred. So at least I was able to tell my unhappy colleague that I had submitted the story to another Walker editor. But it did little good. His cheerful correspondence stopped cold. This editing business had painful aspects to it, and I soon realized they could not be avoided.

It was especially delightful to discover a strong first novel. One of those, *Abduction from Fort Union*, by Lenore Carroll, proved to be the beginning of her long career as a novelist. She had done some intensive research about old Fort Union, New Mexico, and then had fashioned a gripping story from her explorations.

In fact, I started several people on their way. One of those was my old colleague from the *Billings Gazette*, Gary Svee. He is a six-foot-seven Norwegian giant, one of few people who dwarf me, and his stories were really too piercing to compress into genre western fiction. But he did, somehow, and was eventually published not only by Walker and Company, but by Pocket Books and other houses. I bought his first two novels, *Spirit Wolf*, and *Sanctuary*, both of them built around Indian themes. One dealt with a mythic wolf and an ancient Cheyenne medicine man, while the other dealt with "invisible" Indians slowly starving on the outskirts of a Montana town, unnoticed by the whites there. Svee continues to write penetrating novels that evoke conscience and shame, and tackles topics that would scare off most writers, such as the grim struggle to put food on the table in the bottom of the Great Depression. He has won two Spur Awards and I fully expect him to walk away with several more.

One day a manuscript arrived from a Texan named Sam Brown. He proved to be a genuine cowboy who had spent most of his life working cattle in the Panhandle. He had also been a teacher, and was a cowboy poet. He had written a ranch novel called *The Long Season*, set in Texas in 1884 and involving rival ranchers as well as a young man named Jesse Coldiron who was just getting started. The story was a gem, rich with some of the best-drawn ranching characters I had ever seen, filled with lore, rich in weather, and brimming with suspense. I marveled. It was as close to being a perfect western novel as any I had read. I bought it, and after I had left Walker and Company, he continued to sell his novels to the company. I've lost track of Brown, but I count it my good fortune to start him on his way.

I bought all sorts of novels from all sorts of novelists. I bought a couple from old Nelson Nye down in Tucson, "the Baron of Blood and Thunder," and one of the founders of WWA. I steadily bought absorbing novels from Jack Cummings, who had the knack for writing a fast-paced story full of surprises. Walker and Company had a solid library line, and many of the titles I bought were being picked up by mass-market publishers.

I turned to my own work, handwriting *Sam Hook* and then *Richard Lamb*, revising them, and pounding them out on a portable Royal electric. That was grim work, but that quiet woodland atop the continental divide was just the place for serious labor. Since there were few diversions, I was not distracted. Only when I got too lonely did I head for Helena to see friends and stock up on groceries, since I was forty or fifty miles from anywhere. There was never much in the bank, but between the editing checks from Walker, and an occasional advance, I was surviving. I was also living close to the bone, squandering nothing, and maintaining myself in a cabin, a place often visited by coyotes ghosting through the woods, and sometimes by elk and once by a mountain lion. On occasion I did my grocery run at Lincoln, a little timber-bound town on the edge of wilderness; once a gold-mining camp but now populated by a few people who wanted to live at the end of the road, so to speak. Little did I then know that Lincoln was harboring a middle-aged Harvard-educated killer who was also living in a cabin outside of town, but was quietly building and mailing bombs. His name was Ted Kaczynski, and I probably had seen him around town in the cafés or in the little library.

My early novels pursued a theme that became standard in my work. My heroes, far from being youngsters, were older men. These were far more interesting than young men. Both my title characters, Sam Hook, and Richard Lamb, were far from young. Hook was a hardened independent rancher caught in a range war; Lamb was a mountain man, married to a Blackfoot woman, and engaging in trade with the Indians until he ran into trouble with the Army. Most of my protagonists since then have been middle-aged or old. They are far more absorbing then young men full of testosterone. Old men actually think. I was to some extent reflecting my own circumstances, having started writing novels late in life. But there was more to it. I sensed that there were richer stories in older men and women, and I was also carving out a market area for myself. It was well known that most readers of western fiction were older men; why not write stories that would appeal to them?

These Walker and Company stories were picked up by western editor Mary Ann Eckels at Ballantine, and I was pleased to see my novels go into mass market editions. I learned then and there that no matter what the subject of my stories, they would all receive covers that turned them into ranch novels. The Indian trader Richard Lamb has a flowing beard and is dressed in buckskins and moccasins beautifully quilled and beaded by his Blackfoot wife; but on the cover of the Ballantine paperback, he becomes a cowboy, wearing the traditional western hat, a Levi denim jacket and jeans and boots. He sits a western saddle on a stock horse. I chalked it up to the marketing savvy of the mass-market houses at the time, but now I'm not so sure it was savvy at all. Meanwhile, it was great to be getting some additional royalties through these sales. They must have done well: a year or so later, the Ballantine western editor told me I was the second-best selling author in their line. It wasn't an entire living, not even with the steady infusion of editing checks from Walker. But it was a miracle: there I was, surviving on my own, entirely freelance, making it work, paying my bills, paying my rent, and gaining ground month by month.

My agent, Ray Puechner, kept me apprised of a romance he was having with a Texas lady named Barbara Beman. She was spending time in Milwaukee, and Ray, unaccustomed to travel, was wandering off to Texas. Things were looking optimistic for him.

I had met Barbara Beman shortly before I headed west in 1985. It was during one of my periodic trips from Illinois to Milwaukee to see my family. Ray suggested I meet him and his new client, Barbara, at the old Schroeder Hotel in downtown Milwaukee, so I did. I discovered them in the gloomy lobby, waiting for me. There was Ray, wearing a sport coat and looking unusually cheerful, and Olivia de Havilland. It had to be her. It could not possibly be anyone else. I had seen De Havilland in many films, including *Gone With the Wind*. But on closer inspection, this lady was not the actress; this lady was more beautiful, and more elegant, if that was possible, with an oval face framed in soft brown hair, and a slim figure.

Ray had told me about Ms Beman. Like himself, she had wrestled with a drinking problem, recently defeated it, had been dry a year, and was living quietly at a family country home on the Brazos River. She had kept afloat by writing erotic Beeline novels at a thousand dollars a pop, one a month, but now wanted to write other things and had acquired Ray as her agent. After the introductions, during which I was muttering unintelligibly, Ray suggested we repair to the hotel bar, which was even gloomier, and rank with stale tobacco smoke. I followed uneasily, alarm mounting in me with every step. They ordered soft drinks, and so did I, and in due course we were yakking like lifelong pals, a threesome in an empty hotel bar. They proceeded to get drunk. Actually, they proceeded to *act* drunk, becoming more and more relaxed and good humored and comic, even as they sipped ordinary sodas. The two old soaks didn't need booze; they were having a fine time just parked in a saloon. They clearly adored each other, and that feeling extended far beyond the fact that they had wrestled the demons and won. By the time the afternoon waned and we said goodbye—I was leaving shortly for Montana—I thought that Ray wasn't the only male who was in love with Barbara. She had wit, a shrewd grasp of how others thought, and a way of laughing her way past troubles.

According to legend, when Barbara returned to Texas, a pal of hers asked her what Milwaukee looked like. "It looks like a ceiling," Barbara is alleged to have replied. I don't know the truth of it, but I never let truth get in the way of a good story.

Now, in Montana, I found myself invited to their wedding in Milwaukee, and regretted that I could not go. It was, by all accounts, a great wedding, well attended by the mystery and fantasy and western writers who were Ray's clients. And afterward, Barbara began mastering the arcana of operating a successful literary agency under Ray's careful tutelage. It hadn't been her intent to become an agent, but there she was, a full partner with Ray in the enterprise, living in a northern industrial city rather than the wide open sun-swept plains of Texas. She had made a breathtaking leap and was flourishing in an unlikely place. She was an accidental agent, just as I was an accidental novelist. They were frequently in touch: they had manuscripts to sell me, and often it was Barbara who rang me up.

The Western Writers of America convention that year was in Fort Worth, and chaired by Judy Alter. I closed up shop in Montana and drove south, a long trip for someone who hates flying. I was Walker's western editor. It was imperative that I go, and of course I wanted to see my many friends in the organization. Judy Alter had initiated something new: scheduled author-editor meetings, one on one. That was fine with me. I was always looking for great material and knew that sometimes it arrived from an unexpected quarter. A lot of editors showed up at Fort Worth; the western lines of New York publishers were prospering, perhaps spurred on by the triumph of *Lonesome Dove*.

Among those who signed up to have a chat with me was a young couple from Empire, Colorado, named Michael and Kathleen Gear. They were contract archeologists, with advance degrees in the fields of anthropology and sociology. They, too, were living in a cabin in an old Colorado mining town while they pursued their dreams. And currently their dream was to write western fiction, though neither of them at that time had sold anything. About all I could do, upon interviewing these bright young people, was to say yes, I would read their stories; send them to me at Canyon Creek. In due course, after the convention, a UPS truck managed to find me in my lair on the continental divide, and the driver handed off an enormous box that I nearly dropped. I should have used a dolly. I set it on the floor and pried it open and discovered a cache of manuscripts, five hundred pagers, thousand pagers, one after another. They weren't all westerns, either. One, I believe, dealt with Civil War history and slavery. I knew straight off that I could not publish these monsters. I needed genre western material around 60,000 words.

I sat for a while, bewildered. But I had really liked the Gears and had promised them I would read their submissions.

What stared up at me was half a year of reading. What's more, I would have to give priority to submissions that answered Walker's criteria; that is, I would need to read stories that offered some probability of a contract ahead of the Gear material. But I wrote the Gears and explained that I would examine their stories but that it would take a long time.

The Fort Worth convention was a choice one. I remember it fondly because it was there, at the campfire party after the banquet, that I met Jack Schaefer. He had wandered in just to enjoy a collegial moment with his fellow western authors. He lived in Santa Fe and was at an advanced age, but still made it to Fort Worth to receive the Saddleman Award. I remember also that he wore a tweed sport coat and bow tie, and looked more like an Ivy League don than a western novelist. No boots and jeans and Stetsons for this gent. But there he was, the author of what many people felt was the finest western novel ever written. Later I learned that *Shane* embarrassed him; it was romantic, and he felt much better about his realistic novel, *Monte Walsh*. Now, long after his death, a Jack Schaefer Society continues to popularize his work and the films made from his stories.

I also met John Byrne Cooke, Alistair's son, whose massive Simon and Schuster novel, *The Snowblind Moon*, had won the Spur for historical fiction. Another new acquaintance that year was Paul Andrew Hutton, the gifted historian from the University of New Mexico whose biography of General Phil Sheridan had won the nonfiction Spur award.

I had the pleasure of seeing Larry McMurtry pick up a Spur Award for *Lonesome Dove*. I have always approved of making the Spur contest open to nonmembers. Only if the competition is open to everyone can it be said that a Spur Award represents the best work in the field. McMurtry's Spur Award was a case in point. What if he had been ineligible as a nonmember, and the western novel that had won a Pulitzer Prize could not win a Spur? It would have resulted in a great embarrassment for WWA.

The book signing at that convention was held in a outdoor gallery area of the Fort Worth stockyard, and it attracted a lot of people. Western fiction was obviously big in Fort Worth, a legendary Texas cowtown. It was there I met another hero of mine, Ben Capps, who was also well advanced in years but happily in attendance in a blue shirt and red suspenders. I bought, and he signed for me, one of his classics, *The Trail to Ogallala*. Later I obtained *The White Man's Road*. Both of these were considered to be literature, and dealt with themes that were only then starting to be explored. These are titles that deservedly belong on the all-time best western fiction lists.

I returned home to a lot of reading. One of the manuscripts was by an affable Texan named Fred Bean. He'd been a lot of things in his life, including the manager of an Oldsmobile dealership. (The moment he called car salesmen "fender lizards," he won my undying esteem.) Now he was burning to become a western novelist. I read his novel, which showed real promise, and thought that with a few pointers Bean might make the grade. So I wrote him a lengthy critique and shipped the manuscript back. Later he told me that the critique, which he pinned on his wall, was the turning point for him. He consulted it, and did eventually sell a story to Walker after I was gone. We became fast friends, and I always looked forward to seeing him at the conventions.

I did read the Gear manuscripts one by one and drafted rather critiques. I could manage only one at a time but I was inspired to go ahead because I found myself reading remarkable material. The Gears weren't hesitant to explore the meaning of things, and sometimes the story would stop while the characters would debate, say, the whole issue of slavery in a sort of Socratic dialogue. I suggested that the dialogues didn't work for several reasons. The story stalled; people didn't converse in that Socratic fashion, and it would be better to make the conflict implicit, seamlessly fostering the debate in the very nature of the action. What characters do, and how they justify their conduct, give meaning to a story without stopping to debate an issue. Gradually, I worked through that pile of manuscripts, still feeling the effort was worthwhile because the Gears were exceptional and eager and gifted. When they did eventually sell—Mike told me they were down to their last seventy-five bucks and about to return to contract archeology again—they made swift progress toward becoming the best-selling and award-winning novelists they are today. They write many of their novels jointly, and have not committed assault and battery upon each other. They even have managed to remain married, which is a testament of some sort to their union.

Later I helped Kathleen repair a novel that just wouldn't sell. It contained two separate but intertwined stories, one dealing with Indians, the other dealing with whites in a wagon train. The problem was, I felt, that she had made the Indians so spiritual, and the whites in the wagon train so evil and perverse, that the two halves of the story just didn't mesh. I suggested that she humanize both groups and get rid of saints and sinners. She did, and soon her story sold. I have always counted it my great fortune to have been the attending physician at the birth of their careers. Over the years, they have often given me a hand up at book sales events, touted my books, and found customers for my novels, and showered me with kindnesses.

7

Restless Times

IN THE FALL OF 1986 I RECEIVED TROUBLING NEWS. My agent, Ray Puechner, was having some medical difficulties. He was losing control of his legs, and was suffering from headaches and backaches and was feeling miserable. I waited and worried, and then early in 1987 the worst sort of news came to me. Ray had cancer. It was inoperable, wrapping itself through his spinal column and penetrating his brain. He and Barbara agreed to some exploratory surgery to scrape the cancer out of his spine, which proved disastrous, and left Ray in brutal pain and on morphine. After that, there was little to do but wait. Ray adopted Barbara's daughter, Glenna, and taught Barbara everything he know about running a literary agency, while she, in turn, took over the day to day operation of the Puechner Agency. For Ray, the end was filled with an agony that not even morphine could subdue.

The marriage had survived barely half a year. Barbara adored Ray, and his death staggered her. Barbara continued the agency, but soon lost some of Ray's clients who simply felt she was not experienced enough and lacked the sort of contacts that Ray had developed throughout the publishing world. I stayed with Barbara. Soon she was making her own editorial contacts in New York. She also began developing her own stable of novelists and sold their material too. Agenting may not have been her life choice, but she soon was on top of the game. Milwaukee was not her favorite place to live, either, but for the time being she settled in.

My friend and editor Sara Ann Freed, at that time with M. Evans, agreed to buy more of my western stories, and for a good price. Barbara had done the negotiating. As I began to sell, I was less dependent on editing fees from Walker, but I was still hesitant to surrender the editing income. I could not live on the advances from library westerns.

When Ray Puechner lived, he urged me to buy my first computer because it would improve my output. It would make writing much easier, he said. I did, buying a Radio Shack model for twelve hundred dollars, a huge investment for me just then. It had its own proprietary operating system and required a Radio Shack printer, which in those days was a percussion variety using a typewriter ribbon. The computer had no hard drive but operated with two large floppies. One contained the operating system and the other was where you saved your work. It was an ordeal to master, and the printers of those times were perverse. But after a lot of experimentation, and despair because I was living in an isolated cabin and had no help at hand, I did master the thing, and my writing did speed up a little. I timidly began composing on the computer, which had a one-color screen, showing green letters on an unlit background. *Dodging Red Cloud* was my first computer-generated novel and also my first Evans novel. It turned out to be a good story, well reviewed, and with a good sale.

But an A-frame cabin on the continental divide was a lonely place. I began driving to Helena more and more, slaking the thirst to be among people again. I didn't have the means to move, and could not surrender my editing position at Walker until I did. But then my luck changed again. I had drafted some proposals for series, and one of these was about a London seaman named Barnaby Skye who had been pressed into the Royal Navy and jumps ship at Fort Vancouver. From there he makes his way into the American interior and becomes a mountain man with two Indian wives and a ferocious horse named Jawbone. Barbara submitted the series idea to various paperback publishers, including Tor, and it was there that I struck gold. Its executive editor, Michael Seidman, liked the series and took a chance on me. I soon had a contract for three Skye novels, at five grand apiece. And I still had some stories to do for M. Evans and the prospect of continuing there.

Even after Barbara's ten percent (the agency was one of the last to switch to a fifteen percent commission) I might survive on my fiction alone if I could get cheap lodging. I wanted to move to Livingston, a gem of a town of 8000 in south-central Montana. It was well-known as a place where writers gathered, and I cherished that. I would find companionship among people who made a literary living. But Livingston, located in a choice corner of the Rockies north of Yellowstone Park, was jammed. A cult called the Church Universal and Triumphant was operating there, and its members had rented or purchased every dwelling and apartment in the whole area. My several explorations there proved futile, and I would need to find a place elsewhere.

I settled on Big Timber, a town of fifteen hundred that was thirty-five miles east of Livingston. It was rather small but amiable, and had a good hotel and restaurant. That was sheep ranching country, sandwiched between an isolated range called the Crazy Mountains, and a spine of the Rockies. Finding a place I could afford was hard there, too, but eventually I landed in a mobile home north of town, on a quiet dirt road. I had never lived in a mobile home, and discovered that this one was reasonably modern and comfortable. But it was fragile, as fragile as the lives of the impoverished people who traditionally spent their lives in such housing, and I had the feeling that a good wind, which was not lacking in that area, would some day sail it away. I moved in the summer of 1987, gave up my position as Walker's western editor, and settled into life on the high plains, with gorgeous blue mountains in view to the west and south.

Jackie Johnson took over as Walker's western editor and continued there until the line was shut down a few years later. I soon realized I was nearly as isolated there as I was on the continental divide. It was a hard grind into town, especially in the winter and spring, when the roads went unplowed or a car could mire in gumbo. But again, work was my salvation. I had a better computer by then, one with a small hard drive and a flashy new word processing program called Word Star. And printers weren't quite so cranky and hard to mesh with computers. I tackled one novel after another, writing obsessively, day and night, knowing that I had to produce and sell fiction at a rate much higher than anything I had done in the past. In all, I wrote five novels for M. Evans and my editor, Sara Ann: *Dodging Red Cloud, Stop, Montana Hitch, Where the River Runs*, and *Fool's Coach*, which won me my first Spur Award. *Where the River Runs* ended up earning more money than any other novel of mine. They were all fairly well reviewed, too.

Barbara Puechner moved to Bethlehem, Pennsylvania, where she could commute to New York, do a day's business and get home again. She had become one of the most successful agents in the field of genre literature, and was selling mystery, fantasy and western material at a good clip. We talked often. Ballantine was still picking up my library hardcovers, so I was getting additional royalties from the paperback versions. But nothing prepared me for the success of *Where the River Runs*. It was a story about a colonel's daughter whose fiancé had vanished in the Northwest while on a treaty-making mission. She talks her father into letting her go upriver to find him, accompanied by a chaperone. In the meantime, Captain Jed Owen, the fiancé, is caught in his own difficulties, some of them the result of his own rash conduct, is forced to winter in what now is Montana, and has no way to return until Spring. The lovers are reunited eventually, but it is a painful reunion. That story was picked up by Tor and enjoyed a good mass-market sale. It went into audio and large-print editions that sold well. The audio, done by Recorded Books, earned me a bundle. Then a South Korean publisher brought out a Korean edition, and next I knew, enormous checks were rolling in. All in all, that little novel earned me about fifty thousand dollars and I am still getting a dribble of cash from it. I had some money in the bank. My life as a novelist was, month by month, becoming more secure, and I could live in less austere circumstances.

In 1989, the last of my M. Evans novels, *Fool's Coach*, won a Spur Award. I remember vividly the call that came from the Spur Awards chairwoman, Jeanne Williams. "Are you sitting down?" she asked. All I know was that I was no longer sitting when I got that news. I was standing, jumping, whirling and dipping. I picked it up at the San Angelo convention, hosted by Elmer Kelton, in 1990.

But back in 1987 I had a larger task. I was beginning the series about Barnaby Skye, the British seaman wandering the Rockies with a belaying pin, two wives and a rank horse. I badly wanted to make it work. Series are the salvation of working novelists. If they are good, they garner a steady readership, which translates into more contracts and a steady income. I believed I had learned enough about storytelling to create a viable series. I had already learned that I simply cannot plot a novel. If I try to put an outline to paper, I end up lost and mired down. Better to think up a memorable protagonist, an equally memorable antagonist, and toss them into an initial conflict and see what happens.

I had already given up thinking of stories in terms of heroes and villains. I prefer the more tragic view of life, in which good people often succumb to weaknesses. People are often driven by harsh circumstance to do things they otherwise wouldn't do. So a hallmark of my writing has been heroes with weaknesses and antagonists who are often driven by their own failings. That has always seemed to ring bells with readers. In a way, I was taking what I had learned from Otis Carney way back at the beginning, and making sure that all my characters were humanized. The antagonist is really the mainspring of the story, and whenever a story bogged, I remembered that the antagonist is the one making things happen.

Tor published the first mass-market Skye novel, *Sun River*, quite swiftly, and the next two came soon after. They were a modest success, nothing dramatic, but certainly not losers. The contract called for 80,000-word stories, but with permission I expanded them to 95,000 or more. The result was an additional buck on the cover price, which meant more royalties for me, and a better chance to win new contracts because the novels were earning far more than their advances. *Bannack* and *The Far Tribes* followed, and did well. I worked out a basic scheme. Skye, a middle-aged guide steeped in lore of the wilds of North America, guides people through danger to their destinations. These were travel stories, with episodic storylines. They worked, in a modest and unspectacular way. Most had net sales in the thirty thousands; a few went into the forty thousands. Skye himself began drawing attention from reviewers. A Brit seaman with a belaying pin was a novelty in western fiction. So was an ugly, murderous horse. So was a hero with two wives, one of them an older and tart-tongued Crow Indian, the other a beautiful and tender Shoshone girl. The novels were helped along by magnificent covers, done by the Spanish artist Royo, and I have always credited that genius with much of my success.

The crunch came when all three had been published but there were few results recorded on the ledgers. I wanted another contract, but the company, Tom Doherty Associates, could not offer one until it had more data. Barbara worked hard at a renewal, but could not get a contract for me. Then, just when I was starting to sweat a little, I got a contract for one more Skye novel, *Yellowstone*. The jury was still out on the series, but they were willing to go with one. So once again Skye was guiding someone into the unknown West, this time a mean-hearted British peer with a large entourage, itching to decimate the whole American bison population. He settles for hauling Skye back to England in chains as a deserter.

As usual, change was occurring. Michael Seidman left Tor; Bob Gleason became the company's editor, and my new editor became Wanda June Alexander. She ably handled *Yellowstone* and the next of my Skye novels, *Bitterroot*. These were lightly edited. Either I was getting better or she had a light hand with the blue pencil. Barbara Puechner was getting contracts for me, mostly from Tor, which was soon to create a new imprint called Forge for its western, mystery, and general fiction lines, and reserve its original name, Tor, for science fiction and fantasy. I was afloat, making a modest living, becoming a working novelist, living the life I had aspired to. I don't quite know how I got there, but there I was.

8

Success At Last

I T NEVER WAS EASY. One of the keys to surviving as a novelist, or as any sort of independent writer for that matter, is to stay out of debt. That can be managed in most respects, but rarely can anyone avoid a mortgage. Another key is to keep cash on hand and resist the temptation to blow it. I began to build up my savings with the goal of being able to survive a year without new publishing income. Another goal is to stay liquid. There were periods lasting several months when I didn't see a nickel come in. A writer has to weather those, and weather disappointing royalty periods. Different publishers have differing royalty schedules, but most report in the late spring and late fall. Another tactic was to keep floating proposals for various new novels. Barbara had been able to narrow the option clauses in my contracts to give me some freedom, and that proved to be vital. Thus, for example, she might be able to narrow an option for my next "work of fiction" to my next "historical novel." We had a certain leeway to probe for new sales, so long as they were in somewhat different realms of literature.

Now, with some books in my background, I began attending writing conferences, and set up as many signings as I could manage. Sometimes I was able to do joint signings. On one occasion Terry Johnston organized a whole book-signing tour through Wyoming and Colorado, and invited several of us to join him.

I learned to work fast, and occasionally I found time to write a spec novel, one without a contract. I wrote several, and if they didn't sell, at least they were out there being circulated by Barbara. When she was satisfied there was nothing more she could do, she sent them back to me, and they ended up on my shelves. Many years later I revised one, a contemporary mystery about cutting horses, and placed it with a modern print-on-demand vanity press. They slapped a grotesque cover on it. The mystery didn't earn more than a few dollars nor did it sell more than a few copies. It was an affirmation: the book didn't have what it took and Barbara was right to give up on it. I pretend I never wrote it, and don't list it as a published credit.

The WWA convention in Sheridan was notable for the number of editors and agents attending. They filled a lot of chairs at the Editors and Agents Panel, and as each arose to tell us what they were looking for, I thought maybe western fiction had a future after all. That may have been the high point of the western revival triggered by *Lonesome Dove* and fueled by another major film and book, *Dances With Wolves*. After that, the usual erosion set in, and only a few years later some of the mass market houses were sharply reducing their western lines.

It had been an easy drive to Sheridan from Big Timber, Montana, except that the motor of my venerable Ford Escort croaked just outside of Hardin and had to be replaced. I rented a car to get to Sheridan. The sort of affluence that might allow me to buy new cars hadn't reached me as yet, but it would come in a few more years when I did buy a brand new Ford Tempo (which was too small and gave me a backache). People often ask me what inspires my writing, and I have a stock reply: money. There are two sorts of financial motivations. The more powerful one is a rapidly declining checkbook balance, but there is also long-term motivation in wanting more cash, more security, and a modicum of comfort.

At the Sheridan book signing we were "treated" to a drum and bugle corps dressed in 1870s cavalry uniforms, and it was so loud that it damaged my hearing even though I had clapped both hands over my ears. My ears rang for days and I've suffered from hearing loss ever since. The winner of the Levi Strauss Saddleman Award that year was Clint Eastwood, and we all waited eagerly for him to fly in and collect it, but the award was ultimately given to an empty chair. We enjoyed a field trip to Eaton's guest ranch, an elegant place near Story, once visited by Queen Elizabeth and Prince Philip. I had learned from some of the staff, who were friends of mine dating clear back to my days at Rancho de la Osa, that the royals required the Eaton Ranch immediately to destroy the toilet seats that had supported the royal buns, which the ranch dutifully did. There was also a fine trip to the Custer Battlefield, which was much more accessible in those days. One could walk among the grave markers. Now, the whole area is fenced off and visitors are herded along approved pathways. At the battlefield cemetery we paused to gather at the grave of University of Oklahoma Professor Walter Campbell, the colorful doyen of western nonfiction, who wrote under the name of Stanley Vestal, and whose work remains a major influence upon the historical literature of the West. Just a few years ago I had occasion to visit that national cemetery once again, to see the grave of Brevet Brigadier General Marcus Reno, who would be the subject of a biographical novel I was working on. There were flowers at his grave, and it is never without decoration.

In Big Timber I bought a home; a run-down cottage, actually. It required a small mortgage, which violated my rule against debt, but I had reserves enough to last well over a year if I got into trouble; reserves enough to cushion myself against disaster. I acquired treasured friends in Big Timber, including cowboy poetess Gwen Petersen, novelist Dee Marvine and her artist husband Don, and magazine writer Jim Overstreet, who sold ranching and rodeo and horse lore material to various publications. Jory and Charlotte Sherman showed up several summers, escaping Missouri heat, living in their camper trailer and doing some trout fishing while writing their series novels. Jory's literary career was rooted in the North Beach area of San Francisco, where he was well known at the City Lights Bookstore. He was one of the Beat writers of that era. He is a natural poet who was writing some of the most lyrical lines I had ever read. The lyricism pervades the narrative segments of his novels and is a hallmark of Jory's work. They had a western series going, I believe *Gunn* was the name of it, and had to ship off a novel a month. Charlotte drafted each story but left it up to Jory to write the erotic scenes in the blank pages she provided for him. The series didn't pay much but offered a steady income, and allowed Jory to work on novels dearer to his heart. Later, Charlotte wrote and sold a romance novel with older women for heroines. My off-and-on fiancee and pal Joyce Coit, of Genoa, Nevada, visited a couple of times, but I had no serious romances brewing during those years.

In the main, I worked on Skye's West novels. Some things about series are easy: I had the central characters down and didn't have to reinvent them. And I had a formula. They were travel novels. Skye and his wives took people into the dangerous and unknown West. Skye was anything but the taciturn western hero. He roared and wept and laughed, and was a binge drinker, and when he got so loaded he was non compos mentis, his tough wives took over and somehow dealt with his unhappy clients. One can scarcely imagine a traditional western with a binge-boozing western hero in it. Neither could one imagine a western hero whose favorite weapon was a belaying pin. I was covering new ground.

But the deeper I plunged into the series, the more my central characters changed on me, and I could not help it. It was as if their deepening history was altering their very natures. Victoria, originally tart-tongued, grew into a shrewd critic of white men's civilization and customs and religion, and was of the opinion that all Europeans were nuts. Skye himself, originally a man with great survival gifts in wilderness, and a raw anger just below his surface, became more reflective, and was soon championing the traditions of the tribes, often defending them against white incursion. It was not planned; my characters were changing, even as I was changing. I was becoming more confident. My researches took me ever deeper into the history of the West, and my initial successes began to quell my anxieties. The series continues even as I write this memoir, and Skye and his family continue to evolve in ways I had never expected. The Skye of my present novels is barely recognizable as the Skye of my early ones. The earlier Skye was more heroic, and recently Victoria has acquired the cajones in the family. But the series goes on and has its own readership. It also gets good reviews, including a starred lead review in *Publishers Weekly* a few years ago.

My hard-working agent, Barbara, sold a new series to Mary Ann Eckels at Ballantine, featuring an Irish doctor in frontier Miles City who was doubling as a part-time sheriff. My hero Santiago Toole was actually an Irish remittance man, sent to the American West by his titled father and fitted out with a profession to avoid all the troubles of primogeniture. The American West was full of such remittance men, so named because of their remittances from across the sea. Only there was no cash on the frontier to support Doctor Toole, who often took his fees in the form of a couple of chickens or a pumpkin pie. He ended up a sheriff, and from there the stories got interesting. When someone pounded on his door wanting help for a gunshot wound, both Sheriff and Doctor Toole were instantly involved.

Those stories turned out to be some of my best fiction to that date. Toole is a wry observer of frontier life, living with a Metis woman, and sometimes patching up the cowboys and scoundrels he just shot. For me these stories were breakthroughs in the area of character. The entire series is rife with unique frontier characters who simply leapt into my head as I was writing them. I don't believe that I have ever created such vivid characters before or since. I have never been afraid to get into the heads of my characters and follow their interior monologues, even though such practices are frowned upon in entertainment fiction and some editors will tell you that interior monologues stop the action. They don't, so long as their inner debates are a part of the story and reveal a character's reasons and intent. In many cases monologues *are* the action. Numerous reviews have commented on the richness of my characterization, and I ascribe it to my habit of following my characters' thoughts. That, rather than depicting idiosyncrasy, is what brings characters to life.

The series did well enough, but suddenly the Ballantine western line got axed. The parent Random House, which also owned Fawcett, saw no reason to maintain two western lines, and the Ballantine one was ash-canned. That sort of thing was not uncommon during the pernicious conglomeration of the publishing industry in the 1980s. Still, the last of the Santiago Toole novels continued as a Fawcett imprint, and the Fawcett editor, Louisa Rudeen, bought a fourth from me. The Toole novels went into two or three reprints, and brought welcome cash into the Wheeler exchequer just when I needed some moolah. I have a fondness for the series. They move into fresh turf, something not easily accomplished in a field that has seen publication of thousands of novels. I've recently acquired reversions of these titles and they will be reprinted by Sunstone Press.

The convention in 1988 would be in San Diego, so I got onto Interstate 15 in Montana and headed south. When I dropped into the Los Angeles basin, the world disappeared in a white haze, and I drove bleakly through white air so thick it obscured buildings only a fraction of a mile away. I thanked Lady Luck that I had not succeeded there and was now living in Montana. Southern California is really a lot of Nowhere, anonymous suburbs sprawled up and down hills, serviced by anonymous shopping centers.

I had first seen San Diego in the 1950s, and it delighted me. Its naval base dominated the waterfront, and it had a great zoo, and gracious homes out on Point Loma. There were orange groves marching up and down the slopes. The old downtown was redolent of history. And just up the coast was the small town of La Jolla, bright and sunlit. Now, as I plowed through the white haze with no clear view of heaven or earth, I saw the same anonymous housing tracts marching up and down slopes once covered with citrus groves. But eventually I found my way to the old hotel where we were meeting, a hotel that was due for the wrecking ball shortly after our sojourn there. Our amiable hosts, Dick House and his colleagues, had a dandy convention awaiting us. The city's summer temperatures were relentlessly pleasant, and we were spending a lot of time out on the hotel's patio.

One of the members I had come to cherish was Robin May, an actor from London. He was also a scholar of the American West, and a specialist on Buffalo Bill Cody. He and Joseph Rosa had done an illustrated book about Cody's sojourn in England with the Wild West. He and my friend Dale Walker shared a love of heroic Victorian poetry and British history, and relished the times they could spend together during the WWA conventions.

One afternoon the Walkers and Robin and I bundled into my car and headed for Tijuana to see the sights. Robin was distinctly nervous, having heard all sorts of horror stories about the border. We made our way across the line without difficulty, and were soon strolling through town. A street photographer with a burro painted with zebra stripes inveigled us and nothing would do but to maneuver Robin into the cart attached to the burro and be photographed. He was a good sport, and vowed to take the Polaroid home to show his family. We bought the usual tourist junk and headed back to the border. Robin grew more and more nervous. There was a famous legend in WWA that involved another Englishman, J. T. Edson, who had attended an earlier convention in El Paso in 1978. He had forgotten his passport, and found himself incarcerated for a while in an Immigration lockup while some members rushed back to the hotel to collect his British passport.

Actually, Robin had two passports with him, and when it came our turn to go through, the border man asked if we were American citizens, and Robin bravely declared he was a subject of Great Britain. With shaking hand, he delivered his passports to the border officer, who swiftly examined them and waved us through. Robin's relief was palpable, and he cheered up considerably en route to our hotel. Robin came to one or two more conventions, but then early Alzheimer's afflicted him, and he could come no more.

Edson, a former canine trainer and handler in the British army, also came to various conventions during that time, sharing a hotel room with voluptuous "secretaries" he brought with him. He churned out westerns by the dozen, and made a good living at it. I discovered at one convention that Edson was about as traditionalist as an Englishman gets, and after that I often would prime the pump a little, just so I could hear him excoriate the nasty politicians who had scuttled the Empire. I read a couple of his westerns, and they were quite solid, but once in a while there would be a bit of dialogue that might sound like this: "Put up your hands, you bloody bloke!" Whatever the case, Edson sold well in this country for years. He finally came to a parting of the ways with WWA, though several people, I included, urged him to stay with us.

As always, after a Western Writers of America convention, I returned to my work recharged and eager to write more. There was always something in those gatherings that inspired me to greater efforts. I don't exactly know what it was. We were the Untouchables of American literature, and that had much to do with it. The Brahmins at *The New York Times Book Review* didn't know we existed. If we had not been outcasts, we would not have drawn so close. With each convention my circle of writing friends widened and often resulted in lively correspondence in those pre-internet days.

I fashioned some series proposals for Barbara Puechner to sell. I had fathomed that I do best when I come up with something quite different from the run-of-the-mill western. I also fathomed that traditional, or genre western fiction, was simply exhausted and most of the original mass-market paperbacks were not distinguishable from thousands of westerns that had come and gone over the decades. Westerns had not changed much since Owen Wister's 1902 ranching novel, *The Virginian*, which is credited by most scholars as being the first modern western. Most of them dealt with ranching themes. Some dealt with lawmen, or mining camps, or the frontier military. Very few dealt with relationships of whites and Indians. There were stray stories about wagon trains, railroads, gamblers, and outlaws. Most were set in the latter part of the 19th century, and that is the period most often required by the publishers of western lines. At those conventions, one editor after another would rise, say that he—or she—was looking for action stories set in the thirty years after the Civil War; that the story should move right along; that these stories were for men, and female characters should be minimal and secondary. Ranch stories were preferred over any other type, but there was room for an occasional mining camp or cavalry yarn, too.

I wanted to try something different. The odd thing about genre western fiction is that it scarcely touched upon the actual West and its history. Genre westerns had been ritualized as gunfighter novels, yet there was a whole wide world these stories ignored. I set to work on a proposal that would be a radical departure in many respects. First, it would deal with the buffalo robe trade of the 1840s, the decade following the beaver trapping period, when the West still belonged to the tribes. I knew of no other western fiction dealing the robe trade and its fierce rivalries. The actual history of the trade was dramatic, and ripe for fictionalization. I would call the series The Buffalo Company, and it would involve a St. Louis firm a little like the great enterprise of the Choteau family, which would establish trading posts in the far West to obtain robes from the tribes. There would be several protagonists. At the heart of the company would be Guy Strauss and his son David, the financiers and organizers. There would be several other partners, most of them out in the field, operating the posts and ensuring that the robes reached St. Louis safely.

By that time, Barbara Puechner submitted the proposal to Pinnacle, and much to my delight, the company bought the series. Wally Exman became my editor. He was quiet, bookish, a veteran of the publishing world, and he had a wry wit. The series name was changed to The Rocky Mountain Company, and at $5,500 per hundred-thousand-word book there would not be much money in it, or so I imagined. (The future would bring some happy surprises to me.) But it was breakthrough fiction. I was on fresh turf. I was also moving in new social directions. As far as anyone knew, my heroes, Guy and David Strauss, were the first Jewish protagonists in the fiction of the West. It was a chance to open new worlds. Once again, Barbara had come through for me.

By that time, Bob Gleason had become my Tor editor, although he farmed out the actual editing to an anonymous woman in Maryland, and he did only the acquiring. Eventually I did sell a new series about a frontier editor to Tor, but in the meantime Gleason had a proposition in mind. It was time, he said, for me to do a big historical novel as a breakout book. It was time for me to reach a broader readership. I had submitted a proposal for a Skye's West novel in which Skye guides an early Smithsonian expedition into the Dakota badlands to dig up bones, only to run into serious trouble with the Sioux, who regarded the bones of the fossilized giant mammals there as sacred.

Make the hero an experienced wilderness guide, but some-one very different from Skye, he said. Add some romance, and write a hundred-fifty-thousand-word novel for us, and we'll push it and break you out. In those days, that was the whole idea: fashion a break-out novel to launch an author. I did as he suggested. I wrote a proposal about a guide named Rufus Crowe and an early British anthropologist named Candace Huxtable, whose very presence offends her all-male colleagues. I added other sorts who were pioneering in the field of paleontology, archeology, and anthropology. They liked the idea at Tor, issued a handsome contract, and I began researching my first big historical novel. It would eventually be published as *Badlands,* and would cause me considerable pain and soul-searching, but it also would be a large-scale success, with a net sale of 85,000 and some good press. From then on, I would be a novelist reaching a general readership and not just a novelist of the West. It was worth the grief I endured getting there.

9

The Mission

BY THAT TIME I HAD FORMED A GOOD IDEA OF WHAT WESTERN FICTION WAS ABOUT. I had read scores of western novels, was broadly familiar with the living and dead authors who wrote them, had a collection of my favorites, and had acquired some sense of the boundaries. Of course I had seen many films and television episodes also. I had also seen the sharp hostility to the stories of the West that was apparent at the Santa Fe convention and in various studies of western fiction that were cropping up. I was forming my own critical judgment about western fiction, and this was beginning to affect my writing.

For one thing, to put it bluntly, I liked the American West far more than the ritualized stories about it that had preoccupied this country for several generations. Much of that literature really wasn't about the West; it was about males fighting for a piece of turf.

It was also plain to me that genre western fiction was narrow and becoming even more so. Prior to World War Two, western fiction was written for general readership: men and women and children. It embraced a wider time frame, more or less from Daniel Boone to the present. Some stories involved cars and airplanes as well as horses and buggies. The earlier fiction was also broader. Mark Twain and Bret Harte had written mining camp novels. There were cavalry novels, wagon train stories, railroad novels, Indian novels, and lawman stories. Much of this had dried up by the time I arrived, and at the WWA conventions of the eighties and early nineties, editors were sharply limiting what they would be willing to purchase from us.

This narrowing of western fiction was due to the phenomenal influence of Louis L'Amour, whose massive sales at Bantam became the gold standard for all the mass-market publishers. L'Amour boasted of all the research he did but his stories actually were romanticized ranching novels, usually involving an underdog pitted against a sinister combination of older villains. L'Amour claimed to have walked the land he wrote about, but there was neither a great sense of the land in his novels nor the complex, deep-rooted relationship of settlers to land and weather. They were stories of good guys and bad guys who happened to be wandering around an unsettled country. If he did much research, it didn't show up in his writing.

Partially because of self-promotion and partly because L'Amour did develop a market for this sort of story, he came to dominate the whole field for a third of a century, and the result was that every other mass-market house tried to imitate Bantam's line, and even the library western lines were heavily influenced by L'Amour. The effect of all this was a precipitous narrowing of western fiction. No longer was it written for a general audience. It became men's fiction, and it was loaded with "action," a word that really meant a lot of shooting, ambushes, fist fights, and various other forms of mayhem such as whippings, torture, sniping, lynching, high noon shootouts and gang warfare. These testosterone-laden stories not only drove away general audiences but even drove away many male readers, who found them tiresome. How many males actually devour stories of gunfights and fistfights and gang warfare? By the time I began to write these novels, editors were relentlessly whittling down the field to whatever L'Amour was writing and Bantam was publishing.

That never was very appetizing to me. All the while I was writing my early western novels, I was reading western history and biography. It soon became plain to me that the stories embedded in the real West were richer, more moving, fiercer, sadder, brighter, more incredible than anything that merely sprang from authors' imaginations. I could hardly open a page of western history without discovering astonishing anecdotes and male and female characters that not even the most imaginative western novelist could match. What's more, the real history appealed to both men and women. There were also tonal differences between the real stories of the West, and traditional western fiction. Some of the real stories were heartbreaking. The story might be as simple as a beloved child lost in a blizzard, or as complex as a family grasshoppered off their land and finding no welcome anywhere. The real west was rife with stories of shattered dreams, lost hope, miraculous survival, feckless quests. The real West was a fool's paradise. There were great stories of men digging into barren mines, certain of bonanza gold the next day; of destitute women hunting for a husband of any sort, shape, and condition who might support them. The real West had a way of magnifying human folly and virtue. Wise, courageous people often triumphed. Foolish people, unable to cope with the brutal conditions in a new land, were destroyed. All this was poignant, powerful story material. I had discovered a paradox. Traditional western fiction, once the most powerful genre in the United States, had scarcely touched upon the real West. Thousands of western novels, written by hundreds of novelists, had not even pried open the door.

Here in Montana, there are scores of stories, enough to occupy me for several lifetimes. An acting territorial governor vanished from a river boat and may have been murdered, and then his grieving widow walked the banks of the river for two months looking for his body. Women went mad in isolated cabins. Lynch parties roamed the Missouri breaks to hang alleged rustlers. People tamed wild animals. Wandering divines preached in saloons. River boats snagged and sank on the Missouri. A sheriff supposedly ran a gang of road agents and was eventually lynched. Fur trade posts were caught in the middle of battles between Blackfeet and Crow Indians. Rival mines invaded neighboring claims. Radical miners risked their lives for a living wage and decent working conditions. A cruel winter destroyed about ninety percent of the livestock in the Territory. A miner discovered the world's finest sapphires in a place called Yogo Gulch, and those brilliant blue stones are now in the crown jewels of Great Britain. The Metis, mixed-blood people who rebelled against the crown in Canada, flooded south to find refuge in this state. Lieutenant Colonel George Custer met his doom here, and his subordinates were blamed for the death of his command. A disease-ridden band of friendly Blackfoot Indians was massacred by the army one brutal January day. The copper kings of Butte wrestled each other and the world, and some of them reached new lows of avarice and corruption.

The real West came alive for me on the pages of the history books, alive in ways that made western fiction a shallow imitation of the real story of the westward expansion. I gradually evolved a literary mission, which has grown over the years and has never varied or faltered. I wanted to tell the fabulous stories of the real West rather than just write more novels that imitated the thousands of romantic westerns churned out by hundreds of western writers before my time. I began timidly, often steering a traditional western in a slightly new direction, knowing that I would run into trouble with publishers if I varied their formulas very much. From the beginning, my editors were aware that I was heading away from core western fiction and exploring new things. I remember Sara Ann Freed telling me that I was the most daring of her authors, willing to try stuff, willing to get into trouble.

But I was also discovering something else. The more I strayed from formulaic western fiction, the more the book packagers at the mass-market houses "corrected" the "mistake" of the author by slapping a standard western cover on the novel and writing cover copy that carefully hid the true nature of my story from the public, so that buyers of my stories thought they were getting one thing but were actually getting something else.

My editors actually welcomed some innovation, even though year after year they had stood before the assembled writers at our conventions to tell us what they were looking for. The people who didn't like what I was producing weren't editors; they were those marketing panjandrums and designers in the book factories who prided themselves on putting covers on books that would cause them to leap right out of the pockets on the racks. So they adhered to a hoary tradition. If I wrote a mining camp story, the hero would be dressed as a cowboy. Once I wrote a story about a small-town banker, and the cover featured a gang of cowboys robbing a store even though there was no such episode in the novel. Another time I wrote a novel featuring a heroine, *Dodging Red Cloud*, but the cover displayed an Indian on horseback waving a blanket. If I wrote a story without a gunfight in it, without a revolver being discharged, without a rifle being fired, the covers would announce the story with a line something like this: "The real bloodbath began after they ran out of bullets."

Had you talked to any of those New York packaging people in those years, they would have proudly insisted that their knowledge of what sold and didn't sell was rescuing their western lines; that without traditional western covers, by which they meant ranch romance covers, the books would flop. Their choices were deliberately deceptive. They did not want potential readers to know I had written a story with a heroine, or that I had written one without any gunplay in it. They seemed to be right for a while. But now that western fiction has all but vanished, one can only wonder. Talk to them and they'll give you the reverse argument: with traditional covers they kept western fiction alive long after writers like me, who kept straying out of the fold, had driven off the readership. The mindset that a western must be men's literature and involve "action" and must deal with ranching or law enforcement, and fall within the latter part of the 19th century is alive and well in mass-market houses, and nothing will ever dislodge it, not even the ongoing failure of western lines, one after another. The last western to roll out of a New York mass-market publishing house will have a cowboy with a blazing six-gun on the cover.

It is instructive to look at what happened to mysteries during the same period. Partly because of feminism and the cultural upheavals of the 1970s, the whole mystery genre broadened. For generations, mysteries had fallen into two categories, the cozies and the hard-boiled. The cozies, typified by Agatha Christie, involved a hero or heroine, often an amateur detective, thinking through clues in genteel circumstances to arrive at an understanding of a murder. Hard-boiled mysteries took the detectives into the mean streets. But few, if any, of the detectives or private eyes were women, and the feminists of those periods were clamoring to get through the gates and write mysteries with tough, realistic female detectives.

The end result, after years of broadening the genre, was that there are mysteries for every taste. There are male and female detectives. There are historical mysteries, present-day and futuristic mysteries. These are set anywhere in the world, in any culture. If you want a mystery with a priest as a detective, you can find it. You can find mysteries with a rabbi as a detective. You can find Episcopalian mysteries. You can find mysteries set in ancient Rome. Thanks to Tony Hillerman and Margaret Coel, you can find mysteries set on reservations, mysteries that incorporate tribal belief and religion in the stories.

The field has also embraced true crime and police proce- dural stories. In three decades or so, the whole mystery genre expanded into a smorgasbord, and one can pore through the mys- tery shelves or explore a mystery bookstore and find something to suit one's taste. So both hardcover and mass-market publishers radically expanded the mystery field, and today it is competitive and healthy. But these very same publishers and packagers shrank the western field, narrowed it down to violent men's fiction, and finally drove it nearly out of existence. A genre usually is rescued from decline by plunging in new directions, but when publishers are locked into an obsessive vision of what the genre must be, they will ride it to its doom rather than permit the change that might renew it.

I did not grasp these trends at first. Later I realized that the publishers' marketing and book packaging personnel them- selves were and are the main cause of the decline of western fiction. Western authors themselves were and are the second most important reason for the decline. Our tired, derivative stories won no new readers and drove countless others away. I don't exempt myself from those who failed to inspire critical interest or win new readers.

There are of course many other causes, such as urbaniza- tion and the steady distancing of modern life from the frontier. These days, who cares about trying to cross a swollen river? There are bridges everywhere. But the reality is that the western field was deliberately narrowed, the only exception being the rise of mountain man stories. There had always been a few of these, epitomized by A. B. Guthrie, Jr.'s *The Big Sky*, but it wasn't until Terry Johnston's breakthrough fur trade stories won a reader- ship that a new branch of western fiction began to emerge. Win Blevins' fur trade novels have radically expanded that readership.

But I am viewing all that with the benefit of hindsight. My own view in those early years was narrower.

If the West is rife with material that wasn't being employed in romantic western stories, maybe I could do something about it, though I knew I would be trying the patience of my editors and publishers. Over the years I did try, and I eventually succeeded in publishing novels that ranged far from anything ever before seen in popular western fiction. Whether that affected the decline of the genre I cannot say. I like to think that if it did anything, it established a basis for a new fiction of the American West some time in the future. I can say this: my work has been largely without competition. In some areas, such as my novels of frontier mining, I scarcely have a rival. It's as if I cut loose from the herd, and have been quietly writing in my own world, the West I want to depict, and I am not connected with traditional western fiction now.

At this writing in 2006 I do not know whether my vision of expanding popular western fiction ultimately hurt or helped. The genre has all but vanished, and if in fact expanding the literature of the West was the wrong thing to do, then I have been a spoiler. I must leave it to posterity to say whether my passion wrought good or ill. But my literary mission of writing larger stories about a larger West has never faltered.

The Rocky Mountain Company was the first series I wrote in which I was consciously attempting to expand popular western fiction, although previous novels had quietly attempted to enlarge the noose around the neck of western writing. I did some casual hunting and was unable to find any fiction at all about the buffalo robe trade that flourished in the 1840s and 1850s, although I would not have been surprised to find a novel or two. It astonished me that no author had touched the topic. In the 1840s the giant herds on the western grasslands looked to be an endless source of leather and fur, and there soon was a ready market for meat and tongues and hides. The leather was especially good as drive belts that powered machinery early in the industrial revolution. The soft, well-tanned hides made excellent carriage robes, and could be used to make warm winter coats.

Just as there had been powerful rivals out in the field during the beaver trapping period, so were there bitter adversaries out in the west during the robe trade period, and around this rivalry I could build my stories. But these heroes were not taciturn cowboys handy with a six-gun. They were gifted traders, diplomats, hunters, and builders, and they had a knack for dealing with the tribesmen who came to them with robes and wanted guns, powder, knives, awls, beads and blankets in return.

So I was more or less on virgin ground, and plunged in happily. But along the way, I ran into trouble. No sooner had I gotten into one of these big, 100,000-word novels than I fell ill. It didn't seem serious at first. I had a low-grade fever, steadily under 100 degrees; a mildly sore throat, and utter exhaustion. The leaden weariness was the worst of it. I could barely bestir myself to do the necessary chores to maintain my life. After a few days I went to the family practice doctor in Big Timber. He prescribed antibiotics. They didn't help. Another visit didn't help. Eventually, after realizing he could not help me, he sent me to a throat specialist in Billings. This man examined my throat and prescribed exotic medicines, each one more costly than the previous one. They didn't help. After a few more weeks of ongoing sickness I tried a Billings internist who ran a series of tests for things such as acid reflux and lung disease. He ended up having nothing to offer me.

By then I was desperate. These medical visits had consumed two or three months and a lot of money. I had some high-deductible health insurance, but I was on my own for the first five grand. I was sick. I could barely write. I could barely get myself dressed, feed myself, go to a grocery. I lived alone. There was no one to help me. Writing was my sole income, and I had deadlines to meet. I asked people what to do, but no one had any ideas. I talked to my agent, Barbara Puechner, about getting deadline extensions. She said she would if this didn't clear up soon.

Meanwhile, day by day by day, everything remained the same. Same sore throat. Same fever. I began examining the medical literature. At that time something called Chronic Fatigue Syndrome was garnering publicity, and cures for it were being touted by purveyors of alternative herbal medicines. I tried some of those. They did absolutely nothing for me, confirming for me that there is little of value in most alternative medicines. I suspect that the vague and amorphous Chronic Fatigue Syndrome is an invented disease, the work of marketing geniuses, just the sort to sell piles of pills. One desolate evening I called Win Blevins' wife, Martha Stearn, in Jackson. She was an internist, a friend, and a fellow novelist. She had written a dandy medical thriller. I offered to pay her for a phone interview, but she wouldn't hear of it. So I poured out my story. She asked a few questions, said she had narrowed it down to a couple of possibilities, and then advised me to ask the Billings internist for two tests, one of them being for Epstein-Barr. I thanked her, made another appointment in Billings, and asked the internist for these tests.

He said he would do them because I had asked, but in fact Epstein-Barr had not presented itself—swollen neck glands were a standard symptom and I didn't have them—and he doubted these tests would help. But in fact, the Epstein-Barr test came back positive. Martha Stearn had diagnosed my illness over the phone. Employing her formidable skills, she had done me a kindness I will never forget. At last, I had a name, a known disease. Up until then neither I nor my doctors could even give my ailment a name. The virus causes mono, or "kissing disease,"in college students, who usually shake it off in six weeks to three months. It is rare in people over fifty, and I hadn't done much kissing lately. Now, with a name of my ailment, I was able to do some research. Epstein-Barr was a virus. There was no cure. Some material I got from the National Institutes of Health indicated that it was a rare disease in people my age, and usually burned itself out in twenty-four months. Two years! There was also significant mortality from it, three percent if memory serves me. At last I had a handle on it, but I still faced the problem of making a living.

I gradually worked out a schedule. In the morning I would write for an hour or so, flop onto my bed, and then tackle the writing for another hour in the afternoon. I knew my material was not good; the disease was taking its toll on my creativity, my ability to write bright, cheerful prose. I tried to compensate, to inject humor and cheer, and that helped somewhat. But the prose seemed as leaden to me as my body. I finished a book and it was accepted. Some lifesaving money arrived. I started another, and kept hammering at it. But I was gravely depressed. The days and weeks and months and seasons dragged by without change. Was I witnessing how the rest of my life would spin out?

One year passed, and the second year was swiftly running its course. Once in a while I would seem to get better, and think that at last the end was in sight, only to relapse. I wondered why I was alive. I could not even imagine living like that year after year. And still I wrote. Still I dragged myself into that desk chair and hit the keyboard. Still I struggled to create a story, make my characters come alive, to overcome the sheer dullness that infused every page of those novels. Still I struggled to make a living, put bread in my mouth, pay my mortgage. Still I walked a while each day, forcing my leaden body to get some exercise.

And then one day the phone rang, and it was my friend Jeanne Williams, who had chaired the Spur Award competition that year. One of my M. Evans western novels, *Fool's Coach*, had won a Spur Award, my first. I would need to go to the 1990 Western Writers of America convention in San Angelo to receive it. Sick or not, I would go. Nothing would stop me, and nothing did.

10

Early Harvests

I MADE MY WAY TO SAN ANGELO. Sickness would not stay me and I was long past the contagious stage. Elmer Kelton's fine convention was quartered at the local Holiday Inn, beside the Rio Concho. He had written pulp fiction and then numerous finely-crafted western novels, each employing spare and transparent prose. Although he continued his day job with a live-stock journal, he had steadily climbed to the pinnacle of western writing. He had won more Spur Awards than anyone else, and had won Western Heritage awards from the Cowboy Hall of Fame. He had been honored with the Levi Strauss Saddleman award for lifetime achievement in the field. He was the quintessential professional, a literary hero of Texas, and I welcomed whatever program he might put together.

At that convention I continued to enjoy a friendship

that had begun a year earlier in Portland, with literary agent Nat Sobel. In Portland we had elected not to take a lengthy dinner cruise up the Columbia, and repaired instead to a gazebo inside the hotel bar for some cool drinks and conversation. Nat had started attending WWA conventions a few years earlier, at first out of curiosity, and then because he had come to admire the people he met and the organization that nurtured them. Eventually he became WWA's official agent, putting together anthologies, agenting WWA members, and appearing on panels as an expert on various aspects of selling popular fiction. He numbered several major authors among his clients. He was a trim, decisive, perceptive man with a real eye for talent.

Now, in the early morning cool, we walked along the Rio Concho, renewing the friendship that had begun a year earlier. He thought there might be a fine future for western fiction but only if it could evolve, and only if WWA would evolve and begin to deal with changes that were even then shrinking the market for material about the Old West. He wanted to see some blockbusters, the sort of novel Larry McMurtry had written, the sort of story that would galvanize national interest in the nation's oldest and most beloved form of fiction. He wanted to see WWA do a lot more to nurture fans, maybe doing fan-oriented conventions similar to the Bouchercon that had done so much for mystery writers.

At that gathering I also had a chance to visit with one of my favorite authors, Doc Sonnichsen, of the University of Texas at El Paso. He had written a number of idiosyncratic studies of western history, finely wrought and often wry, if not plain funny. He was an easterner who had landed in the West almost by accident, and had come to love it and then write about it. Anything that was peculiar or bizarre about the West captivated him, and the result was an expertise in whatever was looney in southwestern history. He was also a gracious master of ceremonies, and had occasionally conducted the Spur Awards, slipping an unruly joke or two, among them a ghastly pun or a corny bon mot, into most every introduction. But the hallmark of his work was a hard, skeptical look at western mythology, and a gift for deflating reputations and puncturing gasbags. Little did I know as I visited with him that year, that he would return home to El Paso and die a few hours later. I look up to him still.

Fool's Coach was a traditional western novel set in Montana. In it, a gambler, a retired madam, and a farmer who had struck it rich, team up to escape Virginia City with their wealth intact. They refurbish an ancient stagecoach, get a crew, and try to dodge the road agents who infest the lanes leading from town. I received my award gladly, managed to mutter a few appropriate words, and sat down, the plaque in hand. The real excitement that evening was seeing Max Evans win the Levi Strauss Saddleman Award. Max, author of sixteen works at that time, including *The Rounders*, which became the film starring Henry Fonda and Glenn Ford, was the perfect recipient for high honor, and I rejoiced. There is nothing I like better than to sit down in a bar with Max and his wife Pat, and just listen. Max Evans is one of the greatest raconteurs alive, especially after two or three drinks. I also had the chance to meet James Alexander Thom, whose "easterns," stories of the frontier east of the Mississippi River, were garnering much praise. His *Panther in the Sky*, about the Shawnee chief Tecumseh, was the winner of the Spur Award for longer novels. In those years eight Spurs were given out, half the number given out now, and that made a Spur Award more valuable than it is now.

Back in Montana, with the Spur Award proudly displayed on my office wall, I found myself toiling on my Dakota badlands novel. I drove over to the badlands, which is now a national monument operated by the Park Service, and blotted up its geologic history, the story of its fossils, and the history and religious belief of the Sioux, whose country contained these ancient bones. There were indeed Sioux legends about those giant bones poking from the eroded strata. I scooped up all the books and literature I could find, and felt a novel begin to burgeon in me. The badlands are a lonely, almost sinister place, with serrated stone guarding its secrets from the world. I felt the presence of ancient monsters there, of things unspoken, of dark moods and bloody events.

I also spent time at Bear Butte, the giant black laccolith erupting from the plains north of the Black Hills. This startling black rock is the holiest place of the Sioux and other tribes and central to many creation legends of North American tribes. I sensed its sacredness from the moment I stepped from my car and began to ascend the path that could take me to the top. Along the way, spirit bundles offered in reverence hung from every shrub. I was in a place not dissimilar to a cathedral. Or maybe more. This was a Siouan Mount Olympus, a Mount Ararat, a home of the gods, and I felt it in my very bones. My novel was shaping into a story about origins, which is in a way about religion, and even as I respectfully explored, I was fashioning in my mind a shocking climax to my novel that would occur right there, right in that holy place.

Somewhere along in that period, a miracle happened. My fever left me, my sore throat vanished. The dark red streak on the back of my throat, which I had observed for months, began to fade. For as long as I had been sick, that reddened and swollen flesh back in my gullet was the hallmark of my disease. I began to acquire some energy. Day after day, I got better. I dared to believe that finally, my body had conquered the virus. The elapsed time between the onset and the disappearance of my illness was twenty-two months, just two months short of the maximum span in the literature of the National Institutes of Health. Life brightened. I thanked God. I rejoiced. Maybe I would kiss someone again, which was something I had refrained from doing for two years.

My badlands novel began to bloom once I had worked out my characters and created my hero, a guide named Rufus Crowe. This was far and away the largest novel I had undertaken, and I would need several principal characters and a complex story that would intertwine various themes. It would also be my liberation: I could write about the West that never appeared in genre westerns.

So I had many reasons to rejoice. My reading took me far afield. I examined the whole nascent field of natural history arising in England during those pre-Darwinian days. I read of the struggles of early students of the natural world to make sense of dinosaur and other giant bones. If the world were only six thousand years old, as some interpretations of scripture suggested, where did these monster bones come from? How could they be ancient? How could they be trapped in rock? In England, more than America, these things were fiercely debated, and the church was thundering heresy at those who thought the world might be inconceivably old, and might not conform to the creation story in Genesis.

But there was more. How would the Sioux react to a band of scientists digging up bones in their backyard? How would these ethnocentric white Americans on the expedition respond to the Sioux? Would there be mutual respect, or only dark suspicion, fear of necromancy, and wild flights of malice? There were all those elements in the story.

Writing a huge novel is no small task, even with the help of a computer. I had upgraded to one of those with a primitive hard drive. Word processing programs were getting better. Storage had improved. It was now possible to save a novel on only two or three of those big floppies. Printing was still a nightmare, and I spent hours, maybe days, getting the printer drivers installed and the printers doing what they were supposed to do, meanwhile filling whole wastebaskets with ruined paper. Still, it beat working with a typewriter.

A hundred and thirty-five thousand words later, I printed out my novel and sent it off to my Tor editor, Bob Gleason, who in turn passed it along to a woman on the eastern seaboard for editing. I awaited the result anxiously, meanwhile turning to other projects. Barbara Puechner had been busy selling my proposals, and I had more Skye's West novels to write for Tor, as well as a novel called *The Two Medicine River*, in the Rivers West series that Jory Sherman was packaging for Bantam. Each of those stories was to be built around a western river. I had chosen a rather small river in northern Montana called the Two Medicine, which ran through Blackfoot country, and the proposal was only reluctantly accepted. There were dark and powerful things to write about up in the Blackfoot country, just south of the Canadian line. The commercial intent of the Rivers West series was to focus at first on great rivers, such as the Missouri and Columbia, where there were large populations along the banks who might buy the novels set there. But eventually I was able to get a contract, and it would lead to my one and only Bantam novel. And once again, my novel would soon explore the clash between European and Indian religion, though that had not been my intent when I began. It is simply that all things trace back to religion, and out of religion come the most powerful stories.

But then the edited version of *Badlands* arrived in the mail. I opened it, began to page through the editing, and was soon aware that I was examining a slaughter. I had walked into an abattoir. Page after page had been axed. There were chapters that had been butchered and left for revision. There were pages of notes, of dissatisfactions. There were clumsy rewrites of material the editor had abridged, rewrites that were so crude I didn't want my name attached to them. The more I probed, the worse it seemed. So much had been chopped out that the story no longer made sense to a reader. There are mandatory elements in any story, things that must exist in order for a reader to grasp where the story is going or where it came from. These were missing. Much of the expository material was gone. I did not see how any reader could follow what was left of the novel.

Further examination revealed that the West had been systematically lopped out of the story. I am a strong believer in the idea that landscape and climate and terrain shape a novel, give it a sense of place, and also affect and shape the characters in the story. I had taken care to bring the West alive, to describe the Missouri River, the buttes and plains, the serrated country of the badlands, and the somberness of Bear Butte. All gone. The edited version could just as well have been set in a New Jersey limestone quarry. All in all, between what had been cut altogether and what had been chopped up and rewritten, the novel had shrunk by perhaps forty thousand words.

I fell into a darkness such as I had never experienced. Part of it was simply that I still felt new to fiction, and had accidentally made a career of something that was beyond my competence. Part of it was that I had spent years as an editor, and knew the value of editing, and knew that an author who rejects editing may simply be damaging his own story. On several occasions when I was editing for Walker and Company, I felt that authors had damaged their stories by rejecting my editing. Editors are there for a purpose, which is to make the story more readable, to keep it moving, to ensure that it is believable. Editors are readers' tribunes, the protectors of the public, advocating changes that help readers to grasp the story better. In one case, when an author had rejected my editing, several of my colleagues at Walker wrote him a letter asking him to accept my changes, but they did not prevail. The novel was published as the author required it, and the damage was done. So my whole prejudice was in favor of the editors, not the authors. And here was an editing that had so demolished months of work and care that I could not cope with it.

I wish I could say that I responded in some strong, adult, serene manner. Actually I was reduced to paralysis, a funk so dark that I seriously considered abandoning fiction. I wish I could say I rebounded, found some way to cope, and set to work doing the requested rewrites, but in truth for several days I simply existed in numb disarray, helpless and stupid.

It was, once again, the fear of poverty that rescued me. I had been so long removed from the work force, from the world of résumés and job applications and employment records, that I knew I could never return. Fiction had become my sole living so I had to make this work or there would be nothing in my bank account to pay the mortgage or feed me or insure my car or buy me some shoes. That was my motivation. But the perception that finally helped me right my listing ship was simply ownership. This was my novel; I wrote it. My name would go on it. It didn't belong to that nameless woman in Maryland who had butchered it. It belonged to me. And if it belonged to me, then I would exercise my right to revise it as I chose, and if Tor didn't like that, I would just have to suffer the consequences.

So, wearily, I began with page one, sentence one, and began the long process of putting my story back together, and making it what I truly wanted. I was heartened by what I saw. Here was a unique and powerful novel. I had seen nothing like it. Here was the story of very early anthropologists and paleontologists, long before Darwin had published *The Origin of the Species*, plunging straight into the most sacred heartland of the Sioux. I had a good story.

After recovering my wits, I pushed ahead, rejecting the editing I didn't like, accepting the editing that clearly improved my story, and cutting the grotesque and ungrammatical insertions the Maryland editor had injected into my text. In time I did rework the story, adding and subtracting whole chapters, making sure that the essential narrative elements were all there. And in time I completed a new version and shipped it off to Tor for copyediting. It was accepted and copyedited and improved still more. In fact they liked it and planned to make it my breakout novel, with a lot of publicity and a major tour.

A year or so later it did appear with a fine cover on it. Their cover designers had borrowed its design from *Lonesome Dove* and had spared no expense, using embossed gold foil for the title and byline. They enlarged this into a handsome poster that went out to bookstores across the West. Along with Earl Murray, whose *Song of Wovoka* was being issued at the same time, I did a six-week tour across much of the West. The novel had a net sale of over 85,000 copies. It wasn't widely reviewed, simply because mass-market novels don't command reviews, but that didn't matter. I was getting onto some local distributors' best-seller charts. It wasn't quite a breakout in terms of sales, but it was a breakout in another respect. I had escaped the straitjacket of genre fiction, and afterward I wrote about a larger West.

Some time later I was visiting with my irascible friend Norman Zollinger at one of the western writers conventions, and discovered that he, too, had seen his novel shipped to that woman in Maryland for editing. And he too had gotten back a novel chopped up beyond recognition. But he and I had reacted in different ways. He was tougher than I. He, the retired executive, award-winning novelist, World War Two B-24 crewman who had flown and survived missions through enemy flak, had hotly written "Stet" across the manuscript and sent it on for publication. Stet is the proofreading term for "Let it stand."

11

Helping Hands

O NE OF MY IDIOSYNCRACIES WAS THAT I COULD
NEVER BRING MYSELF TO ASK OTHER WRITERS
FOR BLURBS. I feared that my request would
embarrass them. It is painful to write a blurb for a
friend whose book you don't much care for. So I have
never asked others to blurb my novels for all of the
three decades I have been writing fiction. Very few
blurbs appear on the covers of my books, and those
were not the result of requests from me. One of them,
from Terry Johnston, was an unsolicited gift. I sent him
an unsolicited blurb in return. Another, from Mike and
Kathy Gear, which decorated my *Badlands* novel, had
been garnered by Tor's executive editor Bob Gleason.
There are a few others, all obtained by my editors or
the company's publicists.

One might suppose that was a bad thing. I have

come to realize it is a good thing. Instead of blurbs, my book covers and jackets feature review quotes, which are far more powerful sales tools than blurbs. The public is skeptical of blurbs, rightly believing that these are usually quid pro quos. In many cases, the book browser is not even familiar with the name of the writer offering the endorsement. And once in a while a blurb has a negative impact: a blurb from a disliked author can send the browser sailing away. A cover or jacket loaded with blurbs from all sorts of famous and infamous writers looks more like "who you know" than a critical endorsement. I prefer praise from an objective reviewer, and I suspect my publishers do, too. In recent years most of my novels have a front promotional page consisting of nothing but excerpts of those favorable reviews. My diffidence about collecting blurbs had turned into something better.

I am frequently asked for blurbs, and usually give them. It is my delight to help other novelists, especially those who have just launched their careers on the wings of a fine novel. I also consider it payback. Over the years, I have been repeatedly helped and encouraged. I see my writing career not as some sort of lonely struggle but as a progression through time in which all sorts of people have heartened me, including friends, agents, editors, marketing personnel, wholesalers, and publishers. By blurbing promising books, I am returning some of the favors showered on me. Occasionally it is a struggle to find the right tone. Some books have a great story but are poorly written; other books are elegantly written but the story is dead. So I try to praise what is good in a story and say nothing about its weaknesses.

Somehow, Western Writers of America, Inc., had become a literary home for me, and the friendships I enjoyed there have endured and deepened. I have often wondered what made WWA so special and I have come to an odd conclusion. It is the organization that presides over a disreputable branch of American literature. Indeed, there are plenty of critics and scholars who would deny that western fiction is literature at all. We aren't criticized in New

York and Boston and Los Angeles; we are *ignored*. There is a subtle sense among us that we are pariahs. Somehow that makes WWA more fun and draws us closer together. *We are the underground.*

Bill Gulick recollects that about fifty writers, agents, and publishers' reps gathered in Denver for that first WWA convention in May, 1953. He told Jeanne, his wife, that they might be western writers, but they looked just like people. Later she replied that the new organization should be called the Western Talkers of America. And most of the talking, Gulick says, was done in the bar, or at cocktail parties, or over some late-night booze dished out in the hotel rooms. Nothing has changed since then. Writing is a lonely profession and authors made up for it by doing a year's worth of yakking at the conventions.

From the beginning, the struggle was against the literary "establishment" that had consigned western fiction and nonfiction to oblivion. Nothing much has changed on that score, either. We write in a field that got no respect and still doesn't; got few reviews and still doesn't; got little publicity or promotion from publishers and still doesn't; wasn't available in most bookstores east of the Mississippi and still isn't, and got bad covers and still does.

The bar conversation among all those accomplished scribblers at the conventions was really an education. It took the form of shop talk, not just about writing itself but also about the publishers and editors and agents we dealt with: sneaky contract clauses to watch out for, the magic way to start a novel ("The trouble began when . . ."), those indecipherable royalty reports, advances that never came, promises that were broken, editors who got fired, great beginnings and endings, the best novels Jones ever wrote, stories that misfired, guys who could write a novel in two weeks, the art of keeping afloat during dry spells, jacking up sales in local bookstores, stuff like that. As the conventions rolled by, I found myself eagerly awaiting the next meeting, and seeing all these barstool pals again. At each convention I would also hunker down with my agent and some of my editors and do some business. The personal contact was valuable. They were no longer names at the bottom of letters, they were real people and real friends.

One of the great barstool debates of that period was whether novelists should make their stories as much like films as possible. Loren Estleman once told me that he visualized all of his scenes through a camera lens because films are the dominant form of storytelling, and by making his novels as much like films as he could, he was making them easy to understand and read. And there was also a better chance of a film sale because the stories were structured as films and were loaded with visuals. I found myself heading the opposite direction. Fiction has its unique assets, and I decided to use them. A film is entirely exterior: what viewers see and hear has been recorded by a camera and microphone. But a novel can go anywhere, including the private thoughts of characters. Writers call that getting into the heads of the characters. Good actors can hint at what a character's private thoughts are, but nothing in a movie can match a novel when it comes to depicting the interior life of characters or why they behave as they do. I have simply tried to take advantage of the unique strengths of the medium in which I work, but I am something of a maverick on that one. I no doubt have paid a price: none of my stories have ever been optioned for film. Estleman's stories have been optioned, and I believe his cinematic approach to storytelling is responsible.

Even since literary agent Nat Sobel had shown up at the Fort Worth convention, he had quietly explored the market for western fiction and had taken on some western writers as clients. In 1990 he published a piece in *Roundup Quarterly* that confirmed what we knew. The publishers in New York routinely treated their western authors less well than other authors. He had compiled a list of horrors: a contract for a western he had negotiated had taken nine months to arrive from a publisher, which was the lon-

gest delay he had experienced. The only time he could not negotiate a share of movie rights for his client was when the manuscript
was a western. The worst cover art ever put on one of his clients'
books was slapped on a western. It was a piece of stock western
art that had utterly nothing to do with the story. The worst abuse
he had experienced of the unearned advance clause in a contract
involved a western. A publisher had charged the unearned advance
from one novel against the royalties of another novel.

And get this: a publishing executive friend of Nat's had
awarded his efficient secretary with a new position—that of western editor. The appointment as western editors of inexperienced
East Coast people who know nothing about the West, or westerns,
or even the history of the genre, is an ancient complaint among
western authors. Publishers considered editing western lines to
be an entry-level job, which is one of the reasons western fiction
is all but defunct now. The idea was that bad editing can't hurt
a western. The goal of these editors was to do well enough to
advance up the ladder. The unfamiliarity of the cliff-dwellers of
Gotham with the material they were producing was not limited
to story editors. It affected the copyediting, proofreading, and
promotional material as well. One copy editor, working on a story
of mine that featured an old Indian trader who wore fringed buckskins, was puzzled when I referred to a horse as a buckskin. "A
buckskin is a garment, is it not?" he wrote in the margin.

I heard such complaints at most every convention over
the years, but I was evolving my own solution to the problem.
I was writing about the West, but I was no longer writing genre
westerns. The more I turned to historical and biographical novels
dealing with western material, the more likely I was to receive an
experienced editor who understood my work and enhanced it. We
fashion our own solutions to the dilemmas life throws at us, and
mine was to stop writing horse opera. It was not a hard and fast
decision, and at times I have continued to write genre western
stories because that was how I could earn a living, but for the

most part I found myself in a different environment, with established editors handling my novels.

Apparently my discontent with the editing given *Badlands* got back to the company, because I soon was shifted to Harriet MacDougal, one of the founding partners of Tom Doherty Associates and a senior person in the company. Bob Gleason is an excellent editor and I would have been happy if he had actually edited my work instead of farming it out, but he was limiting himself to acquisitions. I was fortunate to acquire Harriet as my editor because she was busy. I have been blessed with some splendid editors and publishers my entire career, and she was among them. Legend has it that she coined, or perhaps I should say borrowed from radical politics, the informal motto that had inspired Tom Doherty Associates from its inception: "When you hear the word 'literary,' reach for your revolver." I don't know the truth of it, but it sounds right. Harriet's husband, Jim Rigney, who writes as Robert Jordan, was and is a best-selling fantasy novelist. They live in one of the historic quarters of Charleston. Much of Harriet's life is devoted to editing, scheduling, and dealing with the amazing array of operations that involve a top-selling novelist. How she found time for me I could never imagine, and in fact the arrangement didn't last long. Eventually, she realized she could not handle me, and I was switched to another great editor, Dale L. Walker. But she kept track of me. One day, not long ago, I got a phone call from her out of the blue. She had seen the latest *Publishers Weekly*, and discovered a starred lead review of one of my Skye's West novels there, and called to congratulate me many years after I had lost contact with her.

In those years Western Writers of America was a traditional writers guild, and its primary purpose was to make a marketplace for its members. From early Renaissance times, guilds offered employers a pool of skilled labor, and also looked after the rights and privileges of the guild's members. An employer, in turn, could be certain that if he needed skilled artisans he would go to the appropriate guild for capable people. That is because the guilds themselves set standards, and often required a lengthy apprenticeship before granting journeyman status to their members. In short, guilds were the gatekeepers. That was true of WWA, which was formed as a traditional writers guild. It set high standards, and in turn, at each convention editors, agents and publishers arrived, ready to do business. (Active membership required publication "without the financial assistance of the author" of at least three books, or thirty short stories or articles in "nationally recognized publications," or three credited and paid-for screenplays, or nine original teleplays, all actually produced or presented. No material "for which the author did not receive reasonable remuneration" qualified.)

These publishing people from New York were not merely business associates, they were friends, sharing with us the joys and risks of publishing. Many of the book deals Barbara Puechner and I put together during those years were done in the hotel restaurant or bar, where we could negotiate face to face with visiting publishers and editors. The conventions were also a time in which authors found new agents or switched publishers. They could also be a time of cruel disappointments. At her Fort Worth convention, Judy Alter initiated formal interviews with editors and agents. A member could sign up for a brief session and make the pitch. These proved to be more popular with writers than with editors, but the editors gamely participated, and sometimes some business was transacted. For the most part, the editors simply agreed to take a proposal back east with them, and look it over.

In those days before e-mail and the Internet, WWA presidents found themselves immersed in correspondence with members, which was largely done by letter mail. It was the president's responsibility to see that all the ongoing functions of WWA were operating. The presidents checked to make sure the arrangements for the next convention were progressing, that *The Roundup* was being published, that the exchequer had not slid into a sea of red ink, and so on. One of my favorite presidents of that period was Francis Fugate, author of eclectic nonfiction works about the West, including an engaging piece on Arbuckle's coffee, the standard brew of thousands of cattlemen and drovers. In his first presidential column, Fugate invited members to write him, air their complaints and suggestions and visions. He did receive all sorts of mail, and diligently responded to it all, and with great cheer. There were plenty of good ideas rising from the member-ship, often involved with the conduct of the Spur Awards, and some of these were adopted by the directors. There were also the impractical and foolish ideas to contend with. There was an occasional disaffected member, and Francis and other presidents of that period paid close attention to those complaints. WWA was a truly democratic organization, and its officers and board welcomed proposals and ideas. His presidential columns in *The Roundup* continually raised issues that needed attention, not least of which was the organization's chronic poverty. WWA could scarcely publish its magazine, and not much was left over for its other functions.

He devoted several columns to tax law as it applied to writing. Attending WWA conventions was a legitimate business expense for writers of the West, he wrote after talking with the IRS, so long as WWA remained a professional writing organization and there was a solid business purpose in attending. WWA was also a not-for-profit tax-exempt corporation and would stay that way so long as its mission was to foster the literature of the West. His lively columns, in turn, inspired a raft of letters, often contentious or testy, which were dutifully published in the WWA magazine in a special section called Howlin'.

This continuous airing of ideas resulted in an organization that was more effective than it had been before. Fugate was also a recruiter. I found myself on the membership committee and writing the new-member news for *The Roundup*. That was the beginning of my many functions for the organization. I was a board member twice, hosted two conventions, was involved in a commission that sought ways to improve the prestige of the Spur Awards, and was on a committee chaired by Win Blevins that developed and named the Owen Wister Award, after Levi Strauss notified us that it was discontinuing the Saddleman Award. I also served many times as a Spur Awards judge, and once as a consultant in the selection of new Wister Award-winners. I also wrote some of the departmental columns for *The Roundup*, such as Publishers Row, which involved publishing news related to western literature. At one point I was approached by the nominations committee and asked to run for the vice presidency, which in turn would lead to the presidency. That evoked some anguish, and with deepest regrets I turned down the nomination. My sole living was derived from my writing, which was a full-time job, and I could not afford the time a truly committed presidency would require of me. What's more, I knew I had no more executive skills than I had journalistic skills, and I sensed I would not be an effective leader. Still, WWA had become so valuable to me, and intertwined with my life so intensively, that I paid my dues in whatever way I could.

There came the moment, at the end of each convention, when I had to tear myself away from these friends and go home and write. Making a living as a novelist is most of all an ongoing grind, hour by hour and day by day. I lacked the ability to dash off material, and managed to meet my deadlines by applying the seat of my pants to the office chair, as someone famously put it, and wrestling with the half-formed images and characters crowding my mind.

In some respects, as I learned the art of writing fiction, writing became easier. Or at least I had a few more arrows in my quiver. But in a larger sense, it was no easier to write a novel, even after I had written many of them, than it was when I started. Creating a novel is not the same as manufacturing some widget. Each novel is unique. Each involves new characters, human beings

I had to conjure up from my imagination and observation. Each story involved new situations, new emotions I had never before plumbed, new relationships between the characters. Precisely because each novel is entirely new—the very word, *novel*, implies novelty—writing didn't get much easier. What did help was the knowledge that I had occasionally wrestled with similar trouble before. There were, over the years, many thrown-out chapters, many radically changed characters, many alterations of theme—and many delightful surprises. As an author writes a novel, it evolves into something different from the original idea, and this often means that the novel's beginning must be drastically rewritten to conform to the material that creeps in later.

Perhaps my inability to plot or outline complicated these things for me. A novelist who can outline, and then rigorously follows that outline as the story unfolds, probably would avoid the sort of quagmires I routinely got into. On the other hand, I cherish my free-form writing because it brings spontaneity to my characters and also my storyline, and I don't have to wrestle with my characters, or play God with them. I have found that when I mess with my characters and try to turn them into something they aren't, they go on strike. The most helpful thing that deep experience brought me is simply a sense of story. I can usually tell whether something is working. The sooner that my fire alarms start clanging, the easier it is to back out, cut, revise, or ditch the whole idea. That sense of story gradually evolved in me from experience; it is not anything I was born with.

I have rarely seen a novel go smoothly. And I have often written a novel I have to drag out of my ancient brain even when I suppose there isn't a thing in my head. But when these are published, I can't tell the difference between the ones that simply leapt to life and the ones that reminded me of a toothache. There were times when I could write ten or twelve manuscript pages a day and there was less work in it than in carrying a feather; other times when I could hardly manage my minimum quota of six pages and I had to crowbar every sentence out of my work-averse brain. I made myself work. I would sit down and butt my head against the novel no matter how I felt. And somehow I would make my deadline, and look for a paycheck.

Part of the fun of living in Montana was to explore its back country. And in particular, I loved to poke around ghost towns, which were often reduced to a few weathered gray buildings. But at one time those towns had been lively, rich with hope, filled with miners and their families. As I meandered through those ruins I could not help but imagine how life had been in their prime, these bright, sweet islands of civilization in a vast wilderness. Most of them were built around gold or silver mines that soon played out, leaving the ghost of a city behind. I had on several occasions explored the ghost town of Castle, in the Castle Mountains near White Sulphur Springs. It had flourished as a silver mining town but had succumbed to the Panic of 1893, when the bottom fell out of the silver markets. I walked among desolate old buildings, open to the winter winds and summer heat, scaring up elk that lounged there, or watching deer meander through what had once been lively streets. I poked around the mining works, and plucked up bits of black carbonate ore that still littered the ground, and peered down the shaft that had once swallowed the cages taking miners up and down. I listened to the ghosts. I walked the cemetery, looking at the fallen-down stones now covered with cow manure. Few 19th century miners had lived for very long. There were stories in every tumbling home. Stories rising from every crumbling rock foundation. There were lost dreams in the air. In that awful year of 1893, the suddenly unprofitable silver mines all across Montana shut down and within hours, families were packing their wagons and rolling out of towns. Within weeks, flourishing mining towns were empty.

I thought of a western legend that had entranced me for years. Baby Doe Tabor, once the fabulously wealthy queen of Denver, had spent her waning days hanging on to a dead silver mine called the Matchless, living in a Leadville shack and dreaming of other times, filled with remorse and pale hope. The story is so poignant that it had even been turned into a notable American opera. I thought of Castle, which had emptied out almost overnight, and I thought of a tragic heroine like Baby Doe, hanging on to the life she once had, and suddenly I had a whole novel of dreams and loss, one I would call *Cashbox*.

12

All My Children

BY THE EARLY NINETIES I WAS AN ESTABLISHED NOVELIST. I wasn't earning much, but I was surviving in one of the most perilous of all professions. I still thought of myself as an accidental novelist. I still wasn't sure I could earn a living. One of the most heartening indications that I was actually progressing was the tours. Tom Doherty Associates began to spend a lot of promotional money on me. With the publication of *Badlands* in 1992, I went out on my first lengthy tour, which took me through the Rocky Mountain states, Southern California and the Southwest, Texas, Oklahoma, Louisiana, and north through Midwestern states to the Dakotas and back to Montana. I was accompanied by Earl Murray, and we drove my car. I don't like to fly.

A large-scale book tour requires major planning,

and there are publicity firms in Manhattan that do nothing else but put these together. They schedule the bookstore signings, the gigs on radio or television, the visits to distributors, the newspaper interviews, the advertising, and the accommodations. They do press releases and generate hype. It costs a bundle to arrange even a modest tour.

The day arrived when our itinerary was faxed to us, we packed up, and took off. In those days, prior to e-mail, we needed to stay in constant touch with our tour directors and the company publicists, who would keep us posted on schedule changes, cancellations, dinners or luncheons, and anything else of interest, including reviews.

It was obvious that this would be an important tour because for much of it we would have the company's vice president for sales, Ralph Arnote, with us for half of the tour. He knew how to live comfortably in any circumstance, which proved to be more important to a successful tour than I had imagined. He was also a veteran road warrior, full of entertaining stories about things that had gone haywire on other tours. He had read our novels and even had read competitive novels. At the time of my *Badlands* tour Pinnacle was plastering the book racks with my Rocky Mountain Company series, and Ralph took pains to study these. He also gently schooled us in what not to do, what to avoid in conversation, and how to behave. One must never criticize another publisher or author or anything about the distribution system, or complain about buyers. He told us about some authors of his acquaintance who had managed to offend everyone in sight. One such author was being escorted by a distributor through his company's warehouse, where thousands of paperbacks rested on shelves. The author had meandered from stack to stack, picking up and criticizing the books written by rivals. His tour was cut short then and there. I didn't doubt that Arnote was looking over Murray and me, deciding whether we would make good touring prospects for the company.

When we had time to kill, Arnote usually headed for the best hotel in town. There is nothing like the lobby or bar of a grand hotel to while away a spare hour or two between appointments. There is an art to living on the road, to surviving periods when there is no place to catch a nap, no hotel room, no place to eat. There is a whole road lore, and Ralph Arnote taught it to us. But he actually was along to introduce us. He knew most everyone in the book distribution chain in the United States, and we gradually met a large number of buyers, bookstore owners, clerks, distributors, truck drivers, sales reps, and warehouse people.

The truck drivers were especially important: they headed out each day with a load of books and stocked the grocery and drugstore racks. Where they put your book made all the difference in the world. They could bury it behind others, put it low and out of sight, or put it at eye-level, the prime real estate. We often had coffee and doughnuts with the drivers before dawn, and gave the drivers signed books.

We stayed in upscale hotels, often Sheratons and Hiltons, because that sent a signal to local booksellers that the publisher regarded us as important. If we had camped at a Super 8, that too would have sent a signal. Indeed, local people frequently asked us where we were staying, and I came to realize it was a coded question that would tell them how much stock the company put in us. We signed books at distributer warehouses and bookstores, then hopped into my car and drove to the next venue, sometimes deep into the night. It was exhausting but also flattering. I couldn't imagine how a tour could pay back the company. The tour covered our expenses. We moved only a few books at most of the signings.

Arnote introduced us to the sales staffs at bookstores and distributorships with the hope of making our names and faces familiar to them. But I wondered about it. The turnover at most bookstores was so high that in six months no one would know us. To be sure, our very presence stirred some interest in the media, and sometimes bookstores sold some of our signed stock after we had left town. I have never been able to fathom the economics of a large-scale tour, but what I didn't understand, I still enjoyed. We wined and dined like princes, we were treated like dukes, we were flattered and celebrated like kings. I understand tours are a thing of the past now, except for major authors or celebrities who can expect to be mobbed wherever they alight. Certainly they are no longer offered to midlist authors.

Murray and I sought to make the most of our opportunity, and made unscheduled stops wherever we could. We would walk into little bookstores in little towns, introduce ourselves, offer to sign stock, and then head for another little store or newsstand in another little town. Some of those places had never had an author walk though their doors. In all, we visited thirty or forty more bookstores than were on our itinerary.

I made other tours in the years to come, often with Ralph Arnote. The company was doing its best for me; I knew it and I was thankful. Because of the tours I was beginning to feel that I had a future writing fiction. The money they lavished on me was simply a vote of confidence. My advances were inching upward too. They weren't as high as those of various friends and colleagues, but it didn't matter. If my books sold well, I could expect future royalties. I would rather have a smaller advance that is entirely earned out by royalties than a high advance that doesn't earn out. And the steady distributions of royalties every six months are a form of annuity, something I can count on when I am calculating how to stay afloat for one more year. There is a mythology among authors that a high advance guarantees that the company will invest in a lot of publicity in order that the advance will be earned out. I think that is true only of major books by major authors. A novelist of modest achievement, such as I, is much better off with smaller advances that avoid financial disaster and encourage the publisher to offer another contract.

Between the tours, which were cropping up frequently

through most of the nineties, I worked on my historical novels. I had found the sweet place, the realm where I wanted to work, the place where I could write about the West without being confined to shoot-'em-up stories. It was also the realm where I could have hardcover publication, and with it, some attention from reviewers. And I was making a living.

My mother died suddenly in the spring of 1992, and as I hurried back to Wisconsin I was aware of how much she had shaped my life. She had been an English teacher before marrying my father. She had steadily exposed me to literature of all sorts and was not hesitant about correcting my grammar. But mostly I learned English by example. She spoke elegantly, wrote absorbing and flawless letters, and offered lively comments upon whatever books that were currently absorbing her. (I cherish a moment around 1980 when I discovered she was reading Judith Kranz's *Scruples*. She turned to me and said, "I am reading my first dirty book!")

I am sure she was astonished when I began writing westerns. If she had imagined me as a writer of fiction, she probably would have thought I'd be writing stories for the *New Yorker*. In fact, when I was a boy I did write a story and send it to the *New Yorker*, and it was duly returned with a rejection slip. There was nothing in urban Milwaukee that might have inspired a love of the West in me, but there was plenty in my background enticing me to New York. Even now, my literary hero is not a novelist, but an editor, Maxwell Perkins, of Scribners, who discovered and developed the gifts of Ernest Hemingway, Scott Fitzgerald, Thomas Wolfe, Marjorie Kinnan Rawlings, and a host of other writers. Those books and those authors were on the shelves of my parents' home. So were books perfectly designed to lure boys into the realm of fiction, such as Jules Verne's *Twenty Thousand Leagues Under the Sea*. I remember reading *The Yearling* when I was a boy, and was troubled by it. That was long before I had ever heard of Max Perkins. I also found Kathleen Windsor's *Forever Amber* on my parents' shelves, and read it secretly when I was about thirteen.

If it was banned in Boston, that meant I absolutely had to read it. If bluenoses railed, then I had to find out what was so wicked. At about that age I was sent to a boy scout summer camp, took it with me, and got caught reading it with a flashlight in my tent. The punishment was a few dozen barefoot laps around an athletic track. (I never got past the Tenderfoot stage in scouting, being too much of a bookworm.)

My mother had instilled in me the disciplines I would need later in life, and she had never failed to encourage all my editing and writing, perhaps sensing even better than I that I was born to enter those fields. She lived to see *Badlands,* to know all about my extensive tour, and to know that I had a viable career as a novelist, no matter that it had started late in life. I said goodbye to her with love and gratitude.

I had said goodbye to my father much earlier in my life. I was in my mid-thirties when he died of an aneurysm. My adult friendship with him, the time when we came to enjoy each other, had been fleeting. Now, when I returned to Montana, I would begin a novel that would employ my heritage from him, as well as what I had received from my mother. He was a patent attorney. I somehow grew up with an innate understanding of how things work, of machinery, of manufacturing, and such technology as there was in the forties and fifties. My father loved new ways of doing things, new ways of making and refining and milling and digging things. In the industrial city of Milwaukee, he had plenty of business. He was a man who glowed with happiness, and spread his cheer through our household and among his friends. He was a great raconteur, and could soon evoke a good laugh from almost anyone. He had been a young widower, and met my mother in a Little Theater production.

Now I was about to write *Cashbox,* my first frontier mining novel, and that inheritance, that other side of my heritage, came into play at once. I had no trouble grasping how those early mines functioned as I researched frontier mining. I acquired some sort of understanding of crushing, milling, hoisting, blasting, mucking, and all the rest of it. I also had grown up in the last period of steam locomotion, and knew the chuffing and hissing, the ash and smoke, the startling power of steam as it pushed a piston in a cylinder. A mining camp novel was going to be fun.

From writers like Bret Harte and Mark Twain I absorbed what it was like to live in a mining camp perched in the middle of nowhere. Humor was the anodyne for the grief and loss that stalked all the camps. The miners, their families, and all the riff-raff had a roaring good time, because just beyond, in the dark, death and injury stalked.

I had discovered that the archives of the Montana Historical Society in Helena offered a trove of good material, so I hastened over there and soon was plowing through a mound of books, clippings, and articles about Castle, the town I was turning into the fictional *Cashbox*. I don't know of any institution in the West more valuable, more eager to help out, than the Montana Historical Society. By the time I left, I knew a great deal about that old mining town, its life and sudden death, and its ghostly renaissance many years afterward when mining resumed in the 1950s.

Cashbox didn't write itself. I was on new turf. I was also using multiple story lines and several central characters, and each chapter was written from the point of view of one of those characters. Still, the day came when it was time to ship it off to my new Tor/Forge editor, Dale L. Walker. Tom Doherty Associates employs editors who live all over the country, and Dale lived in El Paso, where he had for many years been the director of Texas Western Press. He is a true bookman, thoroughly versed in all branches of literature. He is the foremost Jack London scholar and has put together London collections. He is a formidable historian whose trilogy about the settlement of the West Coast sets the gold standard.

My novel was a modest success, garnered one or two mixed reviews, and didn't sell well in spite of a lengthy tour and good advertising. I attempted to jack up sales with my own publicity, hiring a publicist to write a canned article about the book and me, to be sent to weeklies and shoppers and papers that do occasionally publish canned releases. We prepared an attractive press release and story and included a photo, and sent these packages out by the hundreds. But the only paper to run the story was my home town weekly. I had poured much of my advance into my publicity, and the failure of that publicity to move even one copy of the novel was a lesson about the perils of book promotion. New York's publishers and publicists are savvy about what succeeds and what doesn't, and when they are cautious about promoting a novel, there usually is good reason. How often I hear authors railing against publishers for not promoting their titles, and to hear authors tell about it, publishers are the dumbest animals in the world. But the joke's on the authors. Most books can't be promoted, even with huge publicity budgets, and publishers are smart not to spend a penny on titles that inspire little interest.

My only solace was that *Cashbox* became a Spur Award finalist. I have a video tape of Texas first lady Laura Bush, who was making the presentation at that El Paso convention, stumbling over my name as she announced the finalists and the winner that year, who was Elmer Kelton.

I did better with my next frontier mining novel, *Goldfield*. I managed to research that one while touring for *Cashbox*. Goldfield, Nevada, had a colorful history and was a great producer of gold in its heyday, which lasted well into the twentieth century. An elderly Wyatt Earp was there for a while. So was Tex Ritter. So were a whole rogue's gallery of Nevada oddballs and crooks and confidence men. So were some lucky fools who got rich in spite of themselves. There's not much left of what once was a city of fifteen thousand, but as usual with mining towns, the Goldfield cemetery told much of the story. There were graves of many hundreds of miners and their families, stones bearing the names of people from every imaginable country. Few of them had lived long. Like most of those old mining cemeteries, the one at Goldfield had been partitioned into precincts. There were plots for Catholics and Protestants, Masons, assorted fraternal organizations, and a special plot for outcasts, mostly Chinese and whores. Heaven, it seems, was pretty thoroughly segregated early in the twentieth century. There was plenty of literature available about Goldfield, and soon a sprawling novel began to ferment in my head, a companion novel for *Cashbox*, but harder, more brutal, and wilder. I was especially taken with a true story about a young Oakland woman who secretly went to Goldfield to find some way to pay off her wastrel husband's gambling debts. She succeeded. I turned her shocking story into fiction, gave her a fictitious name, but stayed close to the bitter realities of her sojourn there.

When I was done with that one, I knew in my bones I had written a good novel. As usual, Tom Doherty Associates did its best for me, sending me out on tour, buying ads, arranging signings wherever I could travel. I thought it might win a Spur Award, but that year the company neglected to enter it, and it was not in competition. I vowed after that to enter my titles myself, and because I did, I won a Spur Award for another book, *Masterson*, in another year when the company neglected to submit any of its western titles for awards. I had learned a valuable lesson: never leave such matters to your publishers. Since then, I have always made my own submissions. Once, just for the entertainment, I submitted one of my novels, *An Obituary for Major Reno*, for a Pulitzer. Anyone, including the author, may enter a book. I hadn't a ghost of a chance but the fantasies I entertained for six months were worth the fifty bucks I had shelled out for the entry fee.

(A Pulitzer *entry* is not a *nomination*, though the terms are often confounded. A true Pulitzer nominee is one of the three finalists that are submitted by the judging juries to the Pulitzer committee for the final selection of the winner. Thus in each category there is one winner and two nominees. I have seen various authors proclaim that their titles are Pulitzer nominees, when all that happened was that their publishers entered the title for consideration. Or maybe they made their own submissions. There is a list of nominees posted on the Pulitzer archival website, as well as the lists of winners for each year. There is also a discussion of the proper nomenclature at the website. I once amused myself checking the claims of various western novelists I know who had declared they were Pulitzer nominees.)

Goldfield got some great reviews. In fact, that novel broke through some sort of barrier, and from then on, I was regularly reviewed by *Kirkus, Library Journal, Publishers Weekly,* and *Booklist*. That improved my sales a great deal: many librarians are guided by the advance reviews, and two good reviews are usually enough to ensure that the title is acquired. And the buyers for bookstores and chains heed the reviews as well.

Of course *Kirkus* is always the toughest and the most iconoclastic, and Loren Estleman used to say that a bad *Kirkus* review is a guarantee that you've written a good book. But if you carry that logic to its conclusion, you must believe a good *Kirkus* review means you have written a bad book. In fact, *Kirkus* has been kinder to me than the other advance review services, so one could argue I've written a lot of bad books.

The review in WWA's own *Roundup* magazine was the one that I treasured most:

> But it is Goldfield itself that is Wheeler's finest character. It is a dirty, noisy, bustling, conglomeration of gamblers, miners, whores, freighters, hucksters, con men, storekeepers, liars, and thieves caught up in a "get-rich-quick" hustle. It is a town of dreams come true and dreams lost. It is the archetypal western boom town where the strong flourish and the weak go broke, and Wheeler describes it with the quiet authority of a writer who knows his subject and the compassion of a man who understands dreams.

I was making a name for myself in a realm of western fiction utterly neglected for decades. The frontier mining camps had vanished from popular and literary fiction. In fact, there hadn't been much since Mark Twain and Bret Harte had worked with the material. The West is dotted with the remains of those towns and the mining works that generated the towns. There are old headframes still standing, venerable stamp mills, amalgamation plants, and rusting iron, but also some of the cottages and mansions, the saloons and boardinghouses that were thrown up in weeks and were abandoned a few years later when the ore ran out. There are astonishing stories in all of them, and I sometimes felt I was tapping into the richest literary gold in the world. I have found more superb material in my mining research than in all of my other research combined.

Oddly, many readers of genre western fiction didn't associate these mining camps with the West. For them, the West was ranching, trail drives, the Indian wars, and in particular, gunmen and outlaws. I know of only one novel done by Louis L'Amour, *Bendigo Shafter*, that centered on mining, and it apparently did not do well because it disappeared from the racks.

By the early nineties, L'Amour's sales had obviously declined and the stories that had once dominated the western bays and racks were being displaced by other authors. Bantam made a major effort to promote a replacement for the king of western fiction. His name was Cameron Judd, and no western author could have asked for better promotion. He was an able novelist of the West, who did have something of L'Amour's magic, but the promotion didn't work. Bantam finally realized you can't just jack someone into becoming a major seller. It must have been a humbling experience for Bantam to spend so much and get such unremarkable results. L'Amour did have his own stamp: his novels brimmed from a certain romanticism that he fostered by using Irish and French names for his characters and including a great deal of tenderness in his stories. That romantic form of the western novel was unique and it simply died with L'Amour.

Bantam cut back its western output, and by the mid-nineties other mass-market houses were scaling back as well. The boom wrought by *Lonesome Dove* and *Dances With Wolves* was evaporating. I found myself relatively immune. Through that period I was continuing with my Skye's West series, featuring a hero who was a deserter from the Royal Navy, a binge drinker, a man with two Indian wives, and a man with the most obnoxious horse on earth. That series was surviving while the classic western novel, with the taciturn cowboy devoid of any feeling except anger, was sharply declining. I wrote several more Skye novels, including *Wind River*, in which Skye finds himself a guide for the army, much to his regret; *Sun Dance*, a story about taking some arrogant whites through Sioux country; and *Santa Fe*, in which Skye escorts a flamboyant medicine man and his traveling show to Mexican Santa Fe, and runs into the Comanches. I came to regard *Santa Fe* as one of my most gripping and powerful novels.

But I was running out of material. Each Skye novel consumed a dozen story ideas, because these were episodic travel stories and the events along the road were not necessarily tied together into a unified storyline. And I was running short of characters who might have good reason to travel through the unmapped, unknown West. Because these were original mass-market paperbacks they were not widely reviewed, but here and there, at last, I was beginning to see some confirmation that someone was enjoying them. Sales were not high but were steady. That's how a series works. Readers come back for more if they like what they've read.

In the mid-nineties I thought I had pretty much consumed my material, and I suspected that my Skye novels were looking more and more alike. I finally let Barb Puechner and Tom Doherty Associates know that I couldn't continue the series. It turned out I was wrong. After a hiatus, I started in again, this time with a younger Skye who knew nothing at all about surviving in the North American wilderness. I also shortened the novels to eighty thousand words, which made them more manageable. The second series confused my old readers at first because I was taking the middle-aged Skye back through time to his youth. But eventually they got it straightened out. The series is ongoing, and at this writing I have completed my sixteenth.

13

The Good Life

IN 1992 THE WWA CONVENTION WAS IN JACKSON, WYOMING, HOSTED BY WIN BLEVINS AND JOHN BYRNE COOKE. Win told me later that they balanced each other. Win said he was perhaps too laid back about arrangements while John Cooke was too anxious. Jackson was not a place for people with thin wallets, but we all managed to have a great time. I even went horseback riding after decades of being nowhere near the back of an equine, and after I finally stepped off that placid animal, which was in a dude string, it took a long time to stitch the two halves of me back together. I went riding with Barb Puechner and her daughter, Glenna, and while they kept telling me what a great rider I was, I was telling myself that I wanted off, *right now*. I was about ready to lead my nag back to the stables when we finally got back.

I remember that Jackson convention for several reasons. One is that Loren Estleman met Debi Morgan there and it was plainly love at first sight. They got married one year later on the eve of the next convention in Springdale, Arkansas, to the music of western films. I sat with Barb Puechner enjoying the show. I think the minister was a bit put off by the wild west music at his hitching post, but he completed the hitching in good form. Dale Walker gave the bride away. Debi looked grand. Loren had a few canary feathers on his lips. The processional was "Do Not Forsake Me, Oh, My Darling," that lovely and haunting theme from *High Noon*. And if I remember correctly, the Light Cavalry Overture from *The Lone Ranger* was the recessional music.

At the Spur Awards banquet in Jackson, Win and John had a delight planned for us. Jackson's celebrated lawyer, Gerry Spence, the scourge of corporations, the savior of working girls, would give us a brief address. Spence was a dramatic figure, and he paced back and forth after our dinner was over, speaking extemporaneously about his achievements again vast odds and armies of faceless suits. The trouble began when he didn't quit on time, and the ten-minute talk began to balloon like a bilious belly. On and on he went, deep into the evening. People stirred. Some made a point of rising noisily from their tables, heading for restrooms, and returning. On and on he went, telling his tales of conquest. I watched affable Don Coldsmith finally get up and march out, a scowl on his face. Then Bill Gulick vacated his seat, snapping a loud remark or two en route to the sanctuary of the lobby. Then a dozen others. And from the hallway outside of the banquet hall emerged loud and angry voices. Finally, Win started to wave, got Spence's attention, and ran his finger across his throat, the signal to cut right then and there. Spence slowly deflated and escaped. The awards ceremony didn't wind up until very late in the night, while the wait-staff yawned. Everything in Jackson is high priced and oversized.

John Cooke, Alistair's son, didn't stay long in the western

writing organization, or even in its social circles. He wrote another novel, this one about the detective John Siringo, and did some research on various outlaws. But WWA was not his meat and I think sales of western literature disappointed him. *The Snowblind Moon* had been a Book of the Month Club alternate selection, did well, and went into a Tor paperback edition. (Actually, three books. The novel was too big to stuff into a single mass-market book and got chopped into thirds. I am one of few people who read all of it.)

My friend and compadre W. C. Jameson used to room with him at various conventions. Their lifestyles couldn't have been more opposite. Where W.C. was relaxed in his attire and the way he kept his room, John was precise and exacting. John's shirts hung on hangers two inches apart; John's shoes pointed out from the closet in parade formation. John's side of the closet was as orderly as a military cemetery. If W.C. wasn't quite up to snuff when it came to clothing or toiletries, John set things right. It gave him peace of mind. I've lost touch with John, who lives quietly outside of Jackson, a place he tentatively likes. I hope he is enjoying a good life.

My Bantam Rivers West novel, *The Two Medicine River*, appeared in 1993, and didn't do well. I had written about an obscure but fascinating stream tumbling out of what is now Glacier Park, in the heartland of the Blackfoot country. It was a Romeo and Juliet story involving two half-breeds. The girl, educated in a St. Louis convent, returns to her people and becomes a revered medicine woman of the Blackfeet. The boy turns toward the white world and eventually guides the army on a punitive raid that is known to history as the Baker Massacre. The love of these two runs deep but is never consummated, and when they see each other for the last time, she is dying of a bullet wound from the soldiers. I explored some of the things I love to write about, especially the beliefs of native people and the sharp differences that separate them from the beliefs of Europeans. I thought it was a good story. It did go into an audio edition much later, and lives on as an audio book, even though the original mass market edition has vanished.

Dale Walker was the president of WWA during that period, and wrestling tirelessly with financial and publishing and other troubles within the organization. One of the most alarming was that he had heard nothing from those who were to stage the next convention in Missoula, Montana. He had written several letters asking to be updated on convention plans, the hotel contract, and so on, and had gotten no reply. He had called, and received no answer. It appeared that the person in Missoula who was responsible had apparently abandoned the convention. So Dale took his dilemma to the board, got its consent to go elsewhere in Montana, and called me. We were a few months from a convention and didn't even have a hotel contract. Would I see whether any hotel in my area could accommodate a convention at that late date? That was October. The convention would be the next June. I drove to Billings, found that the Sheraton was booked but the Billings Holiday Inn could handle us if we made a small schedule adjustment, holding our first business breakfast the second, rather than the first, day of our meeting. The Holiday Inn was amazingly helpful. The sales and planning people were so eager and intuitive that I invited them to our Spur Awards banquet, which they enjoyed.

I suddenly found myself putting a convention together in record time. I formed a committee and set people to work on panels, meals, field trips, and all the rest. It proved to be a contentious period, and I was less than diplomatic at times. I needed a few lessons in democracy, as well as in trusting others to do their job. Suffice it to say that we somehow put it together, and the convention was held in Billings, and in the end, it earned a good surplus for the starved treasury. Jory and Charlotte Sherman had come to Big Timber that May to camp at a local campground, fish, and write. I recruited them, and well remember how valiantly they helped stuff all the convention packets. There were piles of material all over my livingroom floor. In the end, we put around three hundred packets together. There were some snafus, but the convention went well enough. We had all sorts of editors on hand, including Greg Tobin, from the Book of the Month Club, and Bantam's retired executive editor Marc Jaffe, who brought his young son to see the reenactment of the Battle of the Little Big Horn. One of the most popular field trips was a tour of old western saloons and watering holes in the area. I had thought it would be a bust, and am delighted to report that I was wrong. We sent a bus to the Buffalo Bill Historical Center in Cody, toured the Custer battlefield, and staged a barn dance and barbeque. My agent Barbara Puechner was there, and she slipped off to do some trout fishing on the Stillwater with Jory Sherman and Fred Bean.

Years earlier I had helped Fred get started. He had submitted a novel to me at Walker, which I had to turn down. But it had merit, and I sent him a two-page critique. He told me later he pinned it to his office wall and that became the turning point. He was the son of a psychology professor at Baylor, and had in innate understanding of human nature, which he incorporated in his novels. Eventually, he put two sons through college with his fiction. He acquired a great agent, Robin Rue, and she kept him glued to the keyboard. He was the most buoyant of people, and always greeted me with a whoop. We became phone pals, and there were times when his knowledge of human nature illumined some problem I was trying to resolve.

In Bethlehem, Barbara Puechner was searching for a different life. She had become an agent as inadvertently as I had become a novelist. When her husband of six months died, she took over, and soon demonstrated her own mastery of the field. But now she was restless. She joined a Unitarian church, looking for something more. On her weekly business trips to Manhattan she often stayed over and worked with Alcoholics Anonymous groups. She maintained an apartment there so she didn't need to rush back to Bethlehem. She made friends with many editors, and often had lunch or dinner with them.

But the agency was palling on her, and she came to a decision: she would put the agency on the back burner, keep serving her existing clients, and move to Southern California, where she had more interests. I don't think she expected what happened. Most of her clients swiftly concluded there is no such thing as a back-burner literary agency; your agent is in all the way or not at all. They left her. She didn't really mind that much, and seemed amused when we talked of it on the phone. I hung on with her, thinking it would work. But in fact, it could not work. She was down to so few clients there were few incentives to continue.

I needed an agent, and turned to my friend Nat Sobel. He loved western fiction, having come to admire the authors he had met at WWA conventions. He was seasoned, powerful, savvy, and capable of launching careers. He was also a man whose wisdom I revered. He had a reputation for closely controlling the product of his clients, and wouldn't market anything he didn't help shape. That, too, appeared to be an asset. He took me on and soon had a fine contract for me: I would write a saga of the California gold rush of 1849. It would be another mining story.

I plunged into the research, and discovered there is a profuse literature of the gold rush and the harrowing ordeal of getting out to that remote place called California, newly conquered by the United States. There were several overland routes, the Panama passage, and also travel clear around Cape Horn. Every route was fraught with peril. On my next book tour I spent time on the western flanks of the Sierras, visiting old gold towns, studying the rivers and canyons where miners had panned gold. I headed for Sacramento where I could see Sutter's Fort, and the way the city flanks the rivers that met nearby. Those lovely oak-dotted meadows, rife with flowers, are among the most serene places on earth.

I read more material that time than ever before, and finally created a story involving two couples; essentially it was a double love story. In one, a restless Midwestern youth abandons his pregnant wife and heads for the goldfields; in the other, a discharged soldier falls in love with a Californio girl, but is torn from her by tradition and religion. Eventually he becomes a successful merchant, supplying goods to the miners. Here was a saga-length story and I eagerly plunged in.. It would be more than a novel about greed and gold. I would explore the tragic fate of the native Californians, known as Californios, who were euchred out of their land and ruined.

Nat asked to see what I was doing, and after completing eighty pages I complied, thinking he would be delighted. His swift reply shocked me. He didn't like any of my characters and didn't much care for the story. Abandon the characters. Pitch this stuff out and start over. He added a postscript: I could make the hero that tinhorn gambler I had employed as a secondary character.

Now, once again, I was plunged into a dark searching of my soul. I was a little better prepared this time, having successfully dealt with the editing of *Badlands*. But once again, I really didn't know what to do. Nat was a successful agent with successful clients and what's more, a good friend. Start over? Make the gambler, who didn't interest me, my central character? I wrestled with that one, and gradually my feelings solidified around the idea of going on with the novel I had in mind, the characters I had given so much thought to, so I concluded to ignore his advice. It was my novel, after all, not his. But that, in itself, would put the two of us on the wrong footing at the very beginning of an agency relationship. His tastes in literature were not mine. If I were to continue with my novel as planned, there could be only one course of action: I would need to resign from his agency. I didn't like that but I saw no way out, and eventually did what I had to do. I wrote Nat that I would continue with the story I had started, and that I would, sadly, need to cease being his client.

The novel bloomed beautifully. It had two poignant love stories. It had tragedy, sadness, triumph, and reconciliation.

Forge published *Sierra* to great advance reviews, the best I had ever seen, such as this from Kirkus:

> With varying results, two young men seek their fortunes in California after America's successful war against Mexico— in another solid historical from the prolific Wheeler. . . . Absorbing and eventful, replete with authoritative details on the mortal risks, primitive conditions, and sometimes rich rewards awaiting those who joined the gold rush to California.

It won the most significant of the fiction Spur Awards, for the Best Novel of the West. It went into an additional printing and mass-market publication. It went into a large-print edition. It earned over twice the original advance, and was my second-most lucrative book. For years, its royalties were so regular they seemed almost an annuity. I received a great deal of mail from people who loved that novel. I even heard from one expert who pointed out that Sutter's Mill, where gold had been discovered, employed a reciprocating saw blade hooked to the water wheel, and not the rotary one described in my novel. (I always dream of writing a flawless novel, but it never happens.)

Nat and I stayed friends, and I always enjoyed visiting with him at subsequent WWA conventions. He doggedly continued, year after year, to awaken New York publishers to the potentials of the authors he had discovered in WWA. If New York publishers remained, and still remain, oblivious to the literature of the West, it is because they weren't listening to Nat.

I needed an agent, and Fred Bean was on the phone every other day or so telling me to check out Robin Rue, who knew how to make things happen. I did, and Fred was right. Robin is now my agent. She examined my work and my career, somehow plowing through some of my novels to get a sense of my writing, even though she worked a breakneck schedule. She asked me what I wanted, where I was going, what I was dreaming of, what I expected, and what might be the pitfalls. I told her I wanted to write about the West in a new way, drawing more from history. I dreamed of seeing the stories of the early West respectable again. I told her that my work was sometimes too slow and needed cutting. I told her I could use more moolah; I wanted to escape from the financial brink at last.

I found myself with a new agent who had a thoroughgoing knowledge of my oeuvre and an eagerness to sell future works. At that time she was running the venerable Anita Diamant agency and Robin sold several of my novels while she was with that firm. But when its owner died and the heirs put it up for sale, Robin resigned, and left for another venue. For a while I stayed with the Diamant Agency's new agent, but he seemed not to know much about my work or purposes, and eventually I decided to see whether Robin and her new associates at Writers House would accept me. They would.

After a hiatus, I was ready to tackle some more Skye novels, and Forge was amenable to the idea. The new series would first be published hardcover, the books would be 80,000 words, and I planned to begin with Skye as a young man. I think Tom Doherty liked the series but he rarely contracted far ahead, always wanting to make sure he was not riding a loser. I had come to admire this observant man who quietly showed up at the conventions. Years earlier, he and some colleagues had started their own mass-market company, focusing at first on science fiction and fantasy, and doing well with those lines. But they soon expanded to mysteries and westerns and nonfiction. Often, at the conventions, Tom did his own negotiating. At one convention he came to an agreement with Norman Zollinger, and henceforth Tor/Forge was Zollinger's hard and softcover publisher. I never sold as well as Tom hoped, yet he steadfastly backed me, year in and out. I received contracts, as many as I could handle.

I plunged into the new Skye's West series, now called

Barnaby Skye Novels. I started with Skye's escape at Fort Vancouver from the life he never sought as a pressed seaman, and his plunge into the American interior and a mountain rendezvous with nothing but a belaying pin and the clothes on his back. I discovered that I was creating a somewhat different hero from the one I began with a decade earlier. It wasn't intentional; I had grown as a novelist and aged as well, and the Skye I was rendering as an older author was gentler and not as much in control of his circumstances as the first version of my series hero. Skye has continued to change even as I've aged, and I suspect a reader would find my original Skye to be quite different from the current version. I would not know how to create the original any more; I find I can render characters only through the current lens with which I view the world. My other central characters, Victoria and Mary, have changed as well. Victoria is tougher and more cynical now; Mary more domestic. But when I remember that the series is now twenty years old, what I find remarkable is not the change, but the thread.

There were fine WWA conventions in El Paso in 1995, Albuquerque in 1996, and Cheyenne in 1997. I had come to realize how important the city was to the success of the convention. A good venue added immeasurably to the success of these gatherings. The only truly awful meeting place in my recollection was Oklahoma City in 1991. Its downtown is the deadest place I had ever been in, with few people on the streets day and night, and grim, silent office buildings repelling the eye. Heaven help the wayfarer looking for a good restaurant there, or a good pub, or a theater, or even shops that are open after five or on weekends. I remember that Barb Puechner and I, and a couple of carloads of writers, took off through anonymous precincts built around shabby strip malls, looking for some place to eat. We ended up laughing at our own frustration, because Oklahoma is the Bad Food Capital of the World, and Oklahoma City is as cheery as an opened casket.

No one reads in that city, and bookstores are even rarer there than atheists. We had our book sale that year in a handsome hall at the Cowboy Hall of Fame, but only two or three people ventured in, mostly to greet old friends, and these frigate birds flew away five minutes after they landed. We ended up buying each other's books and silently stealing away before the event ended.

14

Spreading Wings

NORMAN ZOLLINGER WAS ONE OF THE MOST REMARKABLE MEN I'VE EVER MET. He had committed to memory whole Shakespearean plays, not to mention much of Shakespeare's poetry, and could and did recite apropos lines for any occasion. His novels were rich and humane and textured. He had come to New Mexico from Illinois and had absorbed the Southwest so profoundly that he wrote about his adopted land with rich authority. He had, as well, founded the Taos School of Writing, which convened each July at the Taos ski resort in the Sangre de Cristo mountains northeast of Taos. One of those years, he invited me to be a part of the faculty and I accepted, but with some trepidation.

I had done some workshop teaching, enough to know I am a bit slow-witted and not the best of communicators.

I also knew that Zollinger's school had acquired a fine reputation, had a gifted faculty, and was drawing serious students. Its alpine setting in the off-season resort was ideal, and the altitude kept the temperatures comfortable. Norman and his lovely psychologist wife Ginna were nobody's fools when it came to ferreting out potential weaknesses in faculty, but had decided to give me a try. So I found myself doing my first serious teaching.

At his workshops, all students submitted work in advance, and these papers were read beforehand by all the faculty, and then jointly discussed. Whoever might be teaching that student would have the benefit not only of his own critical judgment, but the perceptions of the other instructors as well. I soon learned I wasn't much of a critic; the others dissected the material better than I, and no one did a better job than Norman himself. And yet, each faculty member had his or her own strengths. Some of the material from students was over the edge and suggested personality disorder. We ferreted out that material, discussed it, and were prepared to cope with it. Until I began to teach there, I had not realized that some writers lack balance, to use a gentle phrase, and some write for catharsis.

I express myself better on paper than I do in society, and my social limitations could well affect my ability to teach. Perhaps that is why Norman and Ginna kept a sharp eye on me, sitting in on most of my seminars and round-table discussions. Apparently they were satisfied, because after a while they let me teach unobserved. I especially enjoyed the faculty breakfast meetings apart from the students, when we had free-for-all discussions of the material, the problems raised by some students, the occasional tears or anger or resentment that even the gentlest criticism evoked. There were rules we laid down about being kind, avoiding the "you" accusations, and finding positive things to say. Writing is a tender business but some of the students weren't a bit tender or were simply tactless. Other students were so vulnerable it was impossible to offer them critical help. I came away from the first workshop knowing I had grown; knowing that the experience was more valuable to me, the instructor, than to my students. The pay covered my trip down there so I came out about even financially.

At the last session, the students filled out evaluations of the instructors and participated in a critique of our workshop. It was during those closing hours that I learned, from the evaluations, that I was something of a paradox. Several of the students thought I had the most to offer them, but they felt I had not delivered, and hadn't taught them what was locked within me. To this day I don't know how to overcome that perception of me. It exists even when I think I have given my best to my students. I am haunted by that failure as much as I am by my inability to be a good journalist. I ascribe it simply to shyness; I often swallow the very thoughts I want to express, perhaps because my thoughts are awkward. My wife often corrects my awkward impulsive thoughts, so more and more I resort to the written word, where I have the chance to filter my ideas.

I did well enough so that the Zollingers invited me back to Taos for a second year, and I was more comfortable teaching that time, having learned the ropes. I knew and enjoyed the excellent faculty, all drawn from New Mexico. The second time around I was smitten by one of the students, but it turned out that she was attached and all I could do was enjoy her company while it lasted.

The following year the Zollingers invited Mike and Kathy Gear as instructors, and after that the workshop faded. The Zollingers couldn't subsidize its losses, and it was eventually cancelled. Norman is dead now, and I grieve for my warm, irascible friend, whose literary career began late in life, like my own. His novels live on, greatly admired in his adopted state. His last novel was posthumously published by Tom Doherty, a publisher whose love of literature and those who create it stretches far beyond bottom lines.

One of the last things that Harriet MacDougal did for me as

my editor was to contract for two historical novels which would be marketed in a special way. She had talked it over with the publisher, Tom Doherty, and had made some plans for me. The company had sometimes achieved more success by focusing the entire publicity budget for a book on a small geographical area than by spreading it across the nation. In short, publicity money could be concentrated on a single city for a book that was set there, and result in a larger sale than if the money had been spread thinly elsewhere. She called it a "circus effect." You have your circus parade and a lot of local hoopla, elephants and lions and tigers and trapeze artists, and pretty soon you have a book that is flying off the shelves in that town. The author would go there, do signings, interviews, and jump through hoops. It seemed to be a good idea. Tom Doherty Associates, which was now a part of the Von Holtzbrinck publishing group and associated with St. Martin's, had some success with regional publishing, especially in Texas.

I proposed Albuquerque which had some fascinating history. She countered that there weren't enough readers in Albuquerque, so we settled on Denver. I would write a big, splashy novel about Denver and its environs, and the company would give Denver a real publicity shot when the book appeared. A historical novel about Denver and Colorado would probably be about mining, a field I knew and loved. But I wanted to do more, and in time I developed a theme for this novel. I wanted to write about people whose lives had been demolished and who recreated themselves out of the ashes, who were living second lives. Indeed, *Second Lives* became the title.

And thus I shaped what became my favorite novel, set in Denver's Gilded Age. There was Lorenzo Carthage, the wildest speculator around; Dixie Ball, who won a gold mine and lost it and ended up a chambermaid. There was a tuberculosis patient, Yves Poulenc, who dreamed of becoming a famous dead poet but who got well in spite of himself. I included a failed lawyer, Homer Peabody, trapped in loneliness. And added Cornelia Kimbrough, who wanted only to escape from a rich and barbaric husband, but was thwarted at every turn. All of my characters were caught in disaster. Most of them would find second lives. The novel was my song of faith in the ability of mortals to rebuild ruined lives. It had been inspired, to some degree, by Graham Greene's masterpiece, *The Power and the Glory*, which was a story of a disgraced priest who transforms himself in revolutionary Mexico.

It turned out to be all I had hoped it would be. My characters' lives took unexpected turns, things I never could have imagined, and I was grateful once again that I never plot a story or force characters to do things they wouldn't otherwise do. My editor, Dale Walker, enjoyed the novel, always a good sign. I eagerly awaited publication and the forthcoming publicity circus in Denver. When at last publication approached, I contacted the company's publicity people and told them I was ready for the big push.

"What big push?" they asked.

"Why, the local publicity for the novel," I responded, and explained what had been planned; what Harriet MacDougal, in conjunction with Tom Doherty, had intended.

They had never heard of it. I did finally talk them into setting up a signing in Denver. They were sending Norman Zollinger there and would include me on his tour for a few days. The two of us had a fine time; I liked nothing better than his company, and the sort of soul-searching conversations that good friends treasure. We signed books here and there. Maybe I even sold seven or eight.

So much for the breakout novel, the local publicity blitzkrieg, the well-planned company promotion. My favorite novel withered and died. The reviewers liked it but didn't know what to make of a thematic novel coming from a "western novelist," and the reviews reveal a certain bewilderment with a story that didn't fit any of their categories, least of all western fiction. The story didn't earn much money, won no awards, and gradually vanished into that black hole in outer space where failed novels go. I mourn at its grave.

Well, there were more Skye novels to write, more historicals, more contracts. My new agent, Robin, was doing a great job. I was surviving. Every six months, at royalty time, I received substantial checks because some of the stories had earned out their advances and were paying steadily.

I still had the other novel in the MacDougal contract to write. I was in a mood for breakout books, and if I couldn't count on concentrated local publicity poured upon a novel set locally, as in Denver, then maybe I could try a big contemporary novel. I was able to revise the contract so I could tackle a subject that was riveting people in the West, and especially Montana. Demographers had noted that for years the high plains had been depopulating, and there were many counties in Montana and elsewhere on the plains in which population levels had fallen to what they were before settlement. Economics forced ranches to become larger and larger, driving rural populations off the land. And the towns that supported the ranches withered as well, leaving a vast and lonely grassland. At the same time, there were proposals afloat to restore the high plains to their pre-settlement condition, bring back the great buffalo herds, and also wolves and elk and other wildlife, all of which were better suited to the ecology of the plains than its present uses as ranch land or grain farming or irrigated farming.

There was a good novel in it: people seeking to restore a natural world versus ranchers rooted to the good earth and their way of life. Thus I began work on my only contemporary novel of the West. I studied grasses and ranching and the history of buffalo, and read accounts of how the land looked and felt before it was grazed. I created a story set in the year 2000, a story without villains but rife with conflict between people with different visions and values and ideals. It pitted a visionary billionaire with a dream, against a rancher whose family had pioneered in the area.

I called it *The Buffalo Commons,* employing a term widely in use to describe the vision of a national grassland restored to its original condition, and also a term popularized by East Coast scholars Deborah and Frank Popper, who originated the concept. It was not a novel about good guys and bad guys. It didn't accuse ranchers of ruining the range and it didn't accuse those who wanted environmental change of driving salt-of-the-earth people off the land. Instead, it became a novel about dreams, hopes, fears, and loss. That angered some readers at the extremes, who had divided the world between evil corporate ranching that was wrecking the grasslands and saintly environmentalists in love with buffalo, but the story didn't please some ranching people, either, because my sympathies were with those who hoped to restore the grasslands to their primal condition. One need only consult Amazon's reader comments about the book to see both extremes.

The Buffalo Commons is the only book of mine ever to be boycotted. A certain bookseller disliked it so much he wouldn't stock it. I had a secondary theme in the story involving a feel-good foundation, and I made fun of some of those vacuous foundation types who get fat salaries for doing very little of social worth. For some reason, that bugged the bookseller enough so that the novel vanished from his shelves. The boycott was significant enough in the realm of ideological warfare that a nationally syndicated newspaper columnist, Alston Chase, wrote a piece about it.

The novel suffered one other oddity. The mass-market edition had an elegant cover on it, austere black and white, and on the lower third of the cover was a herd of stampeding buffalo, a blur of motion. But there was something odd about that herd. It consisted not of the American bison, but the South African cape buffalo. Apparently the Manhattan book designers didn't know the difference. I took a lot of ribbing from friends and colleagues, and in fact I enjoyed the joke as much as they did. It was further verification that in some ways, New Yorkers are among the most parochial people on earth.

If I was looking for bestsellerdom, I was approaching it the wrong way. I have always preferred to avoid bizarre characters in my stories. Characters at the extremes of evil and innocence seem unreal to me, though they surely exist in real life. Pollyanna characters are just as repellent to me as weird ones, and just as unbelievable. The problem facing a novelist is to make such extreme people credible, and not simply some villainous creature that the reader knows isn't very plausible. The novelist who employs the bizarre or grotesque to entertain readers is simply using cheap tricks. I can always tell a cheapo novelist without real skills by the weirdness of his characters. A novelist who populates his story with weird characters is simply telling me he isn't a good observer of human nature and is trying to cover his ineptitude with novelty. In *The Buffalo Commons* there were no bizarre people, but plenty of colorful ones drawn from the rural life of the plains. My particular joy is to build compelling novels about ordinary people caught in unusual circumstance.

The reviews were excellent and widespread. I had tapped into an absorbing topic that enlivens conversation anywhere on the plains. It was never much of a seller, but it stays in print so the company must be moving enough copies to keep it active.

The *El Paso Times* summed it up this way:

> Now, with *The Buffalo Commons,* the quiet visionary Wheeler has gone into an area that has long been considered a touchy issue—the environment. . . . *The Buffalo Commons* weaves a story of how good and honorable people clash over values and ideals that are viable from either side. . . . Wheeler warns us that our dreams may become nightmares and that man is the foreigner, the intruder in the land, and for that there is no forgiveness despite all his good deeds.

The West is more than prairies and mountains and cold rivers and canyons. It is more than small towns and agriculture. The West is also great cities, and I wanted to write about one in mortal crisis. Thus was born my San Francisco earthquake novel, *Aftershocks*. I knew the town. I had absorbed it when I lived in the Bay Area. I knew about earthquakes, and how they lurk like some underground dragon in the hearts of all those people on that teetering peninsula. The earthquake of 1906, just a century ago as I write this, was catastrophic. I began my story with the quake itself, and the entire novel deals with its effect on people and the city.

There is an abundance of material about it, and in this case I was able for the first time to employ the still-primitive Internet. The City Museum of San Francisco was online, and I was able to download hundreds of photos and primary-source documents. There were superb histories of the quake and the aftermath. I also discovered two hastily printed and published "instant books" that appeared weeks after the quake, filled with anecdote and photos and drawings, and a lot of misinformation. I got an idea for one of my characters from those books. Both of them had a raft of photos of ruins, and there was scarcely a human being present in any of the photos. Following the custom of the time, the photographers had carefully excluded people from their work. So I decided on a woman photographer who might defy the conventions of 1906, and devote herself to photographing the victims of the quake in all their poignant misery.

The more I delved in, the more excited I became. There were hidden stories and circumstances intertwined with the quake. A corrupt city administration had for years carefully hidden the fact that the rats in the sewers carried bubonic plague, black death, and several people a year were dying from the most dreaded of all plagues. One of my main characters was an architect on the make, whose buildings didn't survive and neither did his reputation. He came to a delicious end, shanghaied and at sea. Another was a Salvation Army girl who had been trying to redeem the Barbary Coast, and who thought the quake was God's wrath upon the wicked city until she found how much the innocent were suffering.

And then there was the real-life General Funston, who took over the city by military decree, abandoning the niceties of civil rights. His soldiers shot alleged looters, who more often than not were simply homeowners searching for their own belongings in the rubble. Funston's engineers were blowing up the city to form fire lines, and it is a good question whether the fire itself, or army explosives, did fatal damage to San Francisco. There were a raft of real-life characters involved in the quake, including Enrico Caruso and John Barrymore and Jack London. The singer eventually escaped on the Oakland ferry and vowed never to return. The actor stayed drunk. Jack and Charmian London sailed across the bay to record the disaster and London wrote a memorable account of what he saw. Great stories at every hand. The book bloomed; it had a natural drama, and all I had to do was move from one character's dilemma to the next. I had high hopes for it.

Forge put a fine jacket on the hardcover, a photo of smouldering Market Street with a giant crack running through the brick pavement. But the company didn't send me out on the road. I suspected they didn't have much hope for it. The reviews were a disaster and the book bombed. I was accused of melodrama and soap opera. San Franciscans especially mocked the book. I was hard put to find anyone who liked it much. I called it my hard-luck novel. But when New Orleans was devastated by Katrina, and its agony played out in eerie similarity to my San Francisco novel, I decided my novel had merit after all, no matter what the critics thought. Real life had provided more melodrama than anything I had included in my novel. A year or two after the publication of *Aftershocks*, I happened to be in San Francisco touring with another novel, and checked all the bookstores I could reach over a two-day period, and found not one copy of my earthquake story. When books croak, they're gone, but recently I put *Aftershocks* back in print, employing the excellent Authors Guild back-in-print program. So the relic is available to anyone who wants to read it. I like it, and to hell with the critics.

I was going out on fewer tours as the years passed. I didn't mind. Tours are hard and delicate work, and their success depends on a lot of variables. There is something wildly flattering about them. One starts with an itinerary carefully worked out by firms in New York that specialize in book tours, and as the tour progresses one receives breathless faxes or e-mails announcing changes of plan. It is fun to be the center of the universe for a few days, stay in splendid hotels, eat superb meals in five-star restaurants with important people, talk to book buyers and distributors, sign copies for readers, meet functionaries up and down the distribution system, go on TV or radio and talk about your book, and then hit the road for the next place.

In truth, there is little economic value in them except for authors who are already bestsellers and can count on moving a few hundred books wherever they alight. There is a lot of rationalization about their value: they generate buzz; the people who work in bookstores get to meet authors and that helps sales; it isn't just the books you sell at a signing, it's the signed books you leave behind that sell after you're gone. Stuff like that.

After decades of observation, I have come to some conclusions. Very little book publicity or advertising works. The big ad in *The New York Times* is just as futile as bookstore stuffers and bookmarks or posters touting your titles. What does work is word of mouth. Someone likes a book and urges others to read it. Word of mouth is not achieved at bookstore signings where people have to ante up a lot of money to buy the book of an obscure author. It is achieved by literally giving that author's books away. The cheapest and best publicity involves signings of free books, and not necessarily at bookstores. Giving away books at book festivals is effective, and a lot cheaper than advertising or tours. If the funds spent on advertising and other promotions for little-known authors were spent simply offering free books to people at various venues, those authors would gain a readership if their work is attractive. If their work isn't attractive, no amount of publicity will bail them out. I believe that publishers should simply give away half of an obscure author's first printing at free bookstore signings, book festivals and other venues, and that this sort of pump-priming is the only type of promotion of obscure authors that will ultimately pay off. It is cheaper than taking seventy percent of that printing back as returns.

15

Trying New Things

BIG TIMBER IS A SLEEPY TOWN OF FIFTEEN HUN-
DRED nestled between the main chain of the
Rockies and an outlying range called the Crazy
Mountains. It has a historic hotel called The Grand,
with a restaurant that serves the best meals in the
region. It is surrounded by legendary ranches, and was
once the center of sheep raising in the state. It has
its share of celebrities. Tom Brokaw's ranch is south
of town. Tom McGuane is his neighbor. For a while,
Brooke Shields had a place nearby, and Michael Keaton
still does. Whoopie Goldberg had a country place for
a while.

    I had a good life there, with fellow writers and
some renowned artists at the core of my social circle. They
were and are cherished friends. But I wasn't meeting com-
panionable single women and there were times when Big

Timber seemed to close in on itself, especially during the hard, long winters. For years I had eyed Livingston, thirty-five miles west, a legendary town of eight thousand chocked with novelists, nonfiction writers, film makers, actors, magazine writers, and people from all over the world. I had wanted to live there from the beginning. It was situated in a corner of the mountains north of Yellowstone Park, and was once the gateway to the park when the Northern Pacific passenger trains were running.

My early efforts to move there were thwarted by crowded conditions wrought by the cult church that had bought Malcolm Forbes's ranch south of Livingston, and also by a lack of funds. But now I was making a comfortable living and had socked away quite a bit of money. I could afford a move. The cult had declined after its guru, Elizabeth Clare Prophet, had predicted the end of the world and it didn't happen. That fateful evening, there had been rollicking end-of-the-world parties in Livingston bars and when midnight passed, there were toasts to the new day. Eventually, Ms. Prophet was diagnosed with Alzheimer's. Some of the cultists had drifted off; there were homes available. I ended up buying an old and historic redbrick house on a tree-lined street filled with other gracious homes. It had about twenty-five hundred square feet, a new addition on the back with a study and bathroom in it, and four bedrooms. I bid on it, bought it in 1996, got a small mortgage that I soon paid off, and moved in at the beginning of 1997. The 1915 house was in serious disrepair, and I spent the next years renovating it. Fortunately I was at the peak of my earning years, and was able to restore that gracious home to its initial elegance. It had nine-foot ceilings and huge windows, giving it radiant light that was especially welcome in the darkness of northern winters.

Livingston is a choice locale, with an historic downtown, a famous restaurant and saloon, and the much-loved Murray Hotel, which was film-maker Sam Peckinpah's favorite hangout. He had a suite on the top floor, and when he was in his cups he was known to shoot holes in the ceiling. The hotel's owner told me she regularly sent him a bill for repairs, and he always paid up. In the seventies, Livingston had become the hangout of such writers as Tom McGuane and Jim Harrison, the offbeat poet and novelist Richard Brautigan, novelist and screenwriter Gatz Hjortsberg, actors Peter Fonda, Jeff Bridges, Dennis Quaid, Margot Kidder, and Warren Oates. McGuane eventually married Laurie Buffett, Jimmy Buffett's sister. Peter Fonda eventually married McGuane's ex, Becky. Adventure writer Tim Cahill settled there, and so did Doug Peacock, celebrated by his pal Edward Abbey as the fictional "Hayduke." In 2001 he married Andrea Bennett, a gifted nonfiction writer, at a ceremony presided over by Peter Matthiessen, who doubles as a Buddhist priest when he is not writing his elegant studies of nature or his novels. While Tom McGuane was writing novels and screenplays such as *Rancho Deluxe* and Jim Harrison was writing *Legends of the Fall*, and Gatz Hjortsberg was churning out movies and books such as *Falling Angel* and Richard Brautigan was writing *Trout Fishing in America*, other writers were settling in the area. One was Alston Chase, a retired philosophy professor pursuing several book ideas that became *Playing God in Yellowstone*, and *In a Dark Wood* and more recently, *Harvard and the Unabomber*. Another was critic and novelist Walter Kirn, who was Margot Kidder's son-in-law for a while. In addition to all that, some eminent artists were basing themselves in Livingston, including Russell Chatham and Janie Camp. Producer and director Joe Camp III settled there, along with his wife, Bridget Kelly.

By the time I arrived, there was only an afterglow, which is still kept alive by a few devotees who have preserved 1970s Livingston in amber. The railroad town had morphed into a literary, film and art town and still is. Its elegant and traditional bookstore, Sax and Fryer, sells the literature of the West in particular, and its amiable proprietor John Fryer generously supports all the local talent. Its other bookstore sells a broader variety of titles, along with records and musical instruments, so Livingston can boast of two fine booksellers.

For decades, Missoula with its great university and a famous writing program had been the center of Montana literature, but that honor had long since passed to Livingston, which has several writers who actually make their entire living from their contributions to magazines or their books. All of this meant that I was plunging into a special place, a small town brimming with kindred spirits, set in an exquisite wilderness, chocked with fine restaurants, busting with great watering holes.

Livingston gets more ink than any comparable town in the country, and much of it celebrates those years back in the seventies and eighties when it was a magical place for hip writers and actors to hang out. Periodically, some newspaper or magazine publishes lists of fashionable Livingston authors, usually starting with Jim Harrison, Tom McGuane, Tim Cahill or Gatz Hjortsberg. Either that or they run a feature about the film people congregated in the vicinity. The wild times are long gone, but the town's odd reputation lingers on. I live quietly and obscurely and escape all those lists of high-profile writers and notables.

I had bought the home of my dreams. I soon paid off the mortgage and now own it free and clear. (I continue to follow the first rule of finance for an independent writer: stay out of debt. Pay no interest. I make no car or house payments.) Renovating that house reduced a pile of royalties to paint and windows and shingles and wiring and plumbing and insulation, but I am now well along with it. I live where I want to be.

The new milieu seemed only to inspire me to greater efforts. I made friends swiftly. I live within a few blocks of several writers, including Tim Cahill, who grew up only a few miles from my birthplace. Tim is the country's the foremost adventure writer. He has been swimming at the North Pole, where he arrived on a Russian nuclear-powered icebreaker, toting a Geiger counter because he had heard rumors about Russian sailors who glow in the dark. The rumors were wrong. There wasn't even a twitch of the needle. He was one of the first to arrive at Jonestown, in British Guiana, where he walked among the bloated bodies of those who drank the arsenic-laced Kool-Aid. He has swum with sharks, crossed Death Valley in midsummer, plunged through African jungles, and floated the upper Amazon past headhunting tribes. He is the only person I've met who had contracted malaria, which made him a celebrity of sorts at the local hospital laboratory.

It didn't take long for word to spread among my friends that I was ensconced in one of the most delightful towns in the West, and pretty soon old pals came knocking. One of them was someone I had known for three decades, dating clear back to my employment as a newsman in Billings. She was Sue Gilluly then; Sue Hart now. Her former husband had been my colleague at the *Gazette*. We had kept in touch over the long years apart, and I had seen her children reach adulthood and leave the nest. She was and is an English professor at Montana State University in Billings, and she specializes in Montana literature. She was close to A. B. Guthrie, Jr. and Dorothy M. Johnson and writes about them with authority. We began renewing an old companionship, and pretty soon there were rose petals on the breeze. I visited her occasionally in Billings; she found good reasons to come to Livingston. She knew most of the writers in town anyway. The life of the accidental novelist was coming together.

In between writing my Skye's West novels, I returned to the big historicals of the West, and my frontier mining interests. I tackled the most famous of all mining bonanzas, the Comstock Lode of Nevada. Here again I was tackling familiar turf, but I knew a good novel of the bonanza period had never been written. Mark Twain had described his sojourn in Virginia City, Nevada, in his memoir of rambling through the West that he called *Roughing It*. He had been a youthful reporter for the *Territorial Enterprise*, and had spent his time writing elaborate hoaxes, some of which backfired on him. Indeed, the day arrived when he made a hasty night exit from the Comstock country, and didn't return for many years. But he was only the sideshow. The Comstock was developed by titans of finance and engineering and mining, and between them all they made the Comstock a legend. I stopped in Nevada, bought out the available literature, consulted about where and how to get some rare books, and began the most intensive research of my literary life. My knowledgeable editor, Dale Walker, steered me to the massive works of Dan De Quille, the pen name of William Wright, boozy newsman, prankster and historian of the Comstock. With Mark Twain's encouragement and help, Wright wrote a spectacular study of the Comstock called *The Big Bonanza*, a book of incalculable value. I ascribe much of my success as a novelist to Walker, whose knowledge of the West and its literature far exceeds my own, and whose editing imposed a discipline on my novels that was sorely needed. He was and is a great editor, in the tradition of Maxwell Perkins.

I evolved a novel that would use historical characters, in all their rainbow shades, with the exception of my narrator and hero, Henry Stoddard, and a few intimates of his. And here I ventured onto new ground. For the first time, I used myself as a figure in a novel. My protagonist, Henry Stoddard, was a son of a rural Wisconsin lawyer, a middling sort who was lost in the crowd, restless and unsettled, who finally heads west to the bright dreams of the Comstock Lode. In Stoddard's anonymous abilities, half way up the ladder, I could draw upon myself, for I was a middling sort as well, easily surpassed by all the bright literary lights, but a jump or two ahead of the hacks. So Stoddard was largely myself. I drew deeply from my own attitudes and beliefs and emotions, and from my strengths and failings, but only a little from my personal history. Stoddard lands a job as a cub reporter on the *Territorial Enterprise*, does well enough but is outshone by Samuel Clemens and William Wright and others. The story evolves from there until Stoddard has reached some success as a mining executive. It was a delight to write about Virginia City, Nevada. Never had such a collection of rogues and geniuses gathered together to work such amazing get-rich schemes, and those rogues eventually bankrupted San Francisco and plunged California into an acute crisis and depression. I had never before written about such giants, and found that it taxed my abilities to catch them on paper.

The novel succeeded in its own slow way, and Forge keeps it in print. The proprietors of the Mark Twain Bookstore in Virginia City tell me they keep it stocked, and advise customers that it is the best depiction of the bonanza years they have on their shelves.

I cherish this review that appeared in the *Amarillo Globe-News*:

> Dick Wheeler must be western literature's most knowledge-able authority on boom towns. No one can quite equal his ability to evoke the feel of grit from dirt streets on one's face . . . and the sounds of loud revelry of drunken miners loose on the town. . . . Wheeler recounts the history of Virginia City from its rude beginnings to its decline, writing in a mostly humorous style by interspersing the comedy with poignant scenes that touch the heart and leave one feeling that good kind of sadness that only great writers can evoke.

My companion, Sue Hart, had projects of her own. She had done a Montana PBS documentary on Ernest Hemingway's sojourns in Montana. He had stayed at a dude ranch above Red Lodge in the thirties and one autumnal day when he was heading for Billings with his friend John Dos Passos, he broke his arm in a car wreck. His seriously fractured arm was saved by the genius of a Billings physician who had studied with the Mayo Brothers, and Hemingway spent several weeks in Billings recuperating and writing a short story based on his experience called "The Gambler, the Nun, and the Radio." All that was duly recorded in Sue's award-winning documentary. She was its associate producer.

Now she and her PBS colleagues were planning a documentary about Montana's delightful novelist and short story writer, Dorothy M. Johnson, who had died in 1984. Johnson's short stories, judged the best in the field by a jury of western writers, had been turned into three major motion pictures, and her other works had won great acclaim. But funding a documentary about her was hard and painful, and the money dribbled in all too slowly. Even so, acting on faith, Sue and her crew were out filming those few living people who remembered Johnson. I watched this evolve with delight and admiration. I had long believed that those who toiled in the most neglected branch of American literature ought to be caught on film before it was too late. Western novelists have never been meat for documentary makers or biographers, with the exception of A. B. Guthrie, Jr., who had a Pulitzer in his pocket. And here was my companion giving life to one of my hopes and dreams.

Sue was deeply rooted in Billings, where she had taught virtually all her life. That was where three of her children lived, and her children's children. That was where her lifelong friends were. That was where she was caring for her father, a retired comptroller for GM who was almost a century old. She was a full professor. Teaching was her passion, and she had become the senior member of the faculty. The lucky students in her Montana lit classes discovered that Sue actually knew some of the authors whose books they were studying, and she embellished her courses with anecdotes and insights those students could receive nowhere else. She had no intention of retiring.

We talked about us. We had an old friendship and many bridges between us in the realm of literature. We shared Montana in all its unique grace. There were differences, too. She is Irish and Catholic; I am descended from New England Puritans. She is outgoing and vivacious and sociable; I am quiet and sometimes not at ease in noisy crowds. She loves large gatherings; I love intimate ones. And so we talked, tentatively at first, thinking about what might the future be, where love might take us, where a union might lead us when we were old and frail.

I knew what I wanted; I wanted to marry this gracious, wise, courageous woman. Life had not been easy for her and that only added to the depth and beauty I beheld. She was, as the lovely old song goes, Someone to watch over me. She would be the one, when we grew old, who would take my hand and smile. Maybe, if I was very lucky, I might be the someone to give her a goodnight kiss and watch over her.

One sweet day I proposed. I had in mind a long-distance marriage. She would continue her complex life in Billings; I would continue my writing life in Livingston, a hundred fifteen miles away. She accepted. I gave her an engagement ring with a gorgeous Montana sapphire in it. There were obstacles ahead; she wished to marry in her church, which meant obtaining an annulment for her, and proof from me that my former wife, Rita, was dead and I was free to marry in Sue's church. But we started things in motion, knowing it would take a year, and eventually it all came together. We were married in November of 2000. That was the beginning of my blue heaven.

In my restless quest to tell the stories of the West in new and better ways, I turned to biographical novels. At that time I didn't know I would have the field virtually to myself. I chose Bat Masterson for my first one. The old frontier lawman and gambler fascinated me. William Barclay Masterson had been a hide-hunter on the frontier, had been involved in a serious scrape with Indians, had been a lawman at various towns, had owned a gambling palace in Denver, had become a gifted aficionado of boxing, and most amazingly, had ended up in New York, where he was a sports editor and columnist for the *Morning Telegraph*.

There at the *Telegraph* was a young lady named Louella Parsons, who loved to corner old Bat and extract stories from him about his days on the frontier. And one of Bat's pals in New York was Damon Runyon, who eventually wrote a short story, "The Idyll of Miss Sarah Brown," around a character named Sky Masterson. And that story eventually was turned into the musical, *Guys and*

Dolls. And Marlon Brando, who actually looked like Bat, played Sky Masterson in the movie version.

There was excellent material available, especially Robert DeArment's demythologizing biography of Bat, which I followed in my novel, and acknowledged in my end notes. The story evolved around a simple idea. Bat and his wife Emma would revisit Bat's past in the West. All this would take place on the eve of Prohibition, which Bat despised. Thus was born an odd, rambling novel in which old Bat and a wistful Emma arrive at various western towns just to evoke some memories. They discover that Dodge City is populated by Bible-belt farmers who are ashamed of its wild past and have obliterated it, even down to tearing away the saloons of Front Street, while Trinidad and Denver no longer have tenderloins and suffer from the good works of the Women's Christian Temperance Union and other dubious reformers. There isn't much known about Emma, and I largely had to invent her, but I was able to include one or two of Bat's friends who were still alive. One of those was irascible Wyatt Earp, who was living with his Josephine in Los Angeles, in semi-poverty.

The novel defied all the conventions of storytelling, but somehow it worked. Cranky, diabetic Bat and his former showgirl wife Emma, meander through Bat's old haunts in the West, running into skeptics and debunkers and drastic change along the way. Out of it comes a portrait of Bat, who was an able lawman and gambler, and who had enjoyed a life in the demimonde.

Forge put a spectacular jacket on the novel, and it was published to the sweet song of great reviews. Before it was over, I even heard from one of Bat's relatives, who thought highly of the novel. It won a Spur Award, my third. It received more reviews than anything I had written to date.

Here are excerpts from a couple of them:

Again depicting characters with frailties as well as heroic qualities, the prolific Wheeler's 25th novel (after

Aftershocks) is a sprightly romp of revisionist western history. In 1919, legendary gunfighter Bat Masterson is a 64-year-old New York City sportswriter who suddenly becomes worried about the inglorious and mostly false reputation he has endured for decades. . . . The journey is a hoot when the old lawman finds the public wants the legend, not the truth. . . .This is classic Wheeler, a solid story about real people told with wit, compassion and a bit of whimsy.
                                                       —Publishers Weekly

Keeping Wheeler's printing history straight is not easy since in a 12-month period he's published *Dark Passage, Aftershocks, Sun Mountain, Flint's Honor,* and now *Masterson,* for a grand total of sharply realistic novels that goes through the roof. This is all good news, however, since Wheeler is among the two or three top living writers of western historicals—if not the best . . . . Strong on character and factual as possible, of course, as it moves smartly along. . . .   *—Kirkus Reviews*

My first biographical novel was a hit. I would do more. But I had other irons in the fire as well, in my endless quest to open up the fiction of the West.

16

First and Last Chapters

MY UNREMITTING PASSION TO WRITE ABOUT A WEST that had been scarcely touched by genre western novels had led me in the mid-nineties to propose a series about a frontier editor. Newspapering was a dangerous profession in the 19th century, and the wise editor kept a revolver in his desk drawer to ward off assassins, people armed with horsewhips, and irate ranchers ready to reduce the editor to pulp. The journalists of that day, often boozy itinerant printers who would arrive in some burg and set up shop for a while, were not inhibited about voicing their opinions, and there was no distinction whatever between news and opinion. The editors not only engaged in wild warfare with each other, but with the public, and not a few of them were driven out of town or shot.

I could not let such a colorful facet of the frontier West go unremarked, and obtained a contract from Tom Doherty Associates to do three novels featuring a fearless young editor and printer named Sam Flint. Like the rest of his wandering breed, he would drift from one new town to another, hauling his Washington hand press and his typecase and paper in a wagon. These were fun to write. Sam usually took the side of some underdog, someone despised or outcast, and arrayed himself against the sinister and rich and powerful, and then would find his life in danger. There was abundant material about early newspapers on the frontier, and I soon had more story ideas than I could ever write about. I completed the three novels, enjoying myself along the way, and titled them after each of Sam Flint's newspapers.

The Forge sales staff didn't like the titles, arguing that *The Silver City Sentinel* made no sense and would win no sales or readers. They had a point. The series stalled, and for a year or more nothing happened and I couldn't seem to get it moving. I finally came up with titles that pleased the sales people: *Flint's Gift*, *Flint's Truth* and *Flint's Honor*, and at last the novels were scheduled and catalogued. But they appeared with minimal jackets and without support, and didn't go anywhere. I sensed that Forge was simply completing its contract. But the final book in the series, *Flint's Honor*, in which Flint sets up shop on the first floor of a bordello in a crowded mining town because there is nowhere else to go, became my best comic novel. The opposing editor is exceptionally villainous, and the owner of the local mines is particularly sinister, while Flint is exceptionally prudish and uncomfortable in his unusual business quarters, fending off stray males not at all interested in something hot off the press.

Publishers Weekly liked the third one, saying it had pizzazz.

I don't suppose the series can be counted a literary or commercial success, but it did succeed in widening the fiction of the West, which remained my goal through my entire literary career. More than ever during the nineties the publishers of other western lines were narrowing western fiction, limiting covers to cowboys brandishing guns, and considering the whole field to be men's literature. Western lines in New York were not considered art or literature, but merely commerce, and as a result western fiction was controlled not by editors but by the sales and marketing staffs, far more than any other genre. Many an editor of a western line in New York would have loved to broaden the field but could not; or if the editor did buy unique stories that didn't fit the orthodoxy, the packagers ruthlessly concealed the real nature of the story in their cover copy and gunman art. I believe that over a couple of generations, this unusual control of western fiction by the packagers in the mass-market houses, rather than editors, proved to be fatal to the genre. It is a paradox of publishing that when a genre fiction line falls into the hands of its marketers, it begins to die. And all through the nineties, we were hearing of the decline of the western novel. Publishers were cutting back; distributors were not buying western fiction in many places. There were ominous clouds lowering over the entire field.

In the mid-nineties the environment for mass-market fiction changed dramatically. The national distribution system imploded. Up until the mid-nineties there were over two hundred magazine and pocketbook distributors servicing their own regions, but by the end of the nineties a handful of giants were distributing across the United States. Before, there were local buyers who were sensitive to local tastes and knew what sold well in Paducah and Des Moines, but now the buyers for the giants ignore local tastes altogether, and focus on best-sellers, letting low-end and midlist books languish. Sales declined. Rack space in groceries and drugstores shrank. The number of bays available in bookstores shrank. Prices of mass-market novels skyrocketed from four or five dollars to six or seven. As any shopper knows, seven dollars will buy two pounds of hamburger. Returns increased as well. Publishers had to cope with net sales of only a third or so of their gross sales. In previous times, a net sale of half to two-thirds was common.

All this had an immediate impact on my sales. I owed much of my success to a buyer at Billings News named Donna Ginter. That distributor serviced the racks at Yellowstone Park. Mrs. Ginter had taken an interest in my books, and each summer she purchased one or two thousand of my novels for distribution in the park. Each spring I spent days in her warehouse signing them all. She once told me that my net sales in Yellowstone ranged from seventy to eighty percent. The park was a giant distribution machine for my novels. People from all over the world went there, found my novels for the first time, and took them home. Mass-market novels are light and durable, and make great companions for campers, or people in park hotel rooms where there is no television. But one day she told me the company had been sold; she was out of a job; the new titles were being bought far up the chain. I was dismayed. One of her last acts was to leave instructions to future buyers about what sold in Yellowstone and what didn't, and she had made a point of including my name. Once again, I was the recipient of amazing kindnesses. I kept in touch with her for several years. She was the best fan I ever had. My mass-market sales never again reached the heights that had been achieved when my novels flooded the park and people took them home.

Still, I was lucky. I was being published by the one house willing to broaden its line; the one house that actually commissioned covers and jackets that were germane to the story, and not wrought from stock western cover art sold to the house on the cheap by itinerant artists carrying portfolios full of acrylic gunmen. As I watched Gotham slow its output of western fiction, I realized that there was nothing I could do about it, nothing any single author could do about it. Giant forces were at work. Preconceptions of what constituted western fiction had fossilized the lines and neither authors nor editors could change them. A public that once enjoyed all sorts of western stories in the *Saturday Evening Post* as well as western movies of all descriptions now thought of them as gunman stories, and that perception could not be altered by one middling novelist wrestling with new forms of the quintessential American literature.

If my goal had been to halt the decline and renew the literature of the West, I had failed utterly. I was a leaf being blown by a gale. But along the way I had benefitted my own career. I was known for offbeat stories. From the start, editors had generously given me some leeway. I had penned all sorts of offbeat stories such as a series about a British deserter from the Royal Navy who was making a home in the wilderness. I was the first novelist to tackle the buffalo robe trade. I had done a unique series about a frontier editor. I had written about mining towns when no one else was touching the material. I had done historical novels, and now was exploring biographical ones. And I was virtually alone in all these fields.

One day I received a call from my friend W. C. Jameson, and his news was shocking. Fred Bean, down in Texas, had been hospitalized briefly and then had died of heart failure. The underlying cause was the failure of his liver, which had finally surrendered to alcohol. I thought back on Fred, and all the conventions when we joyously caught up with each other. Fred, the psychologist's son, had created some of the most intriguing characters I had seen in fiction. But I remembered him especially as the man I called when I needed help, or when I was discouraged, or mystified by the way someone was treating me. Pretty soon Fred's chuckle and cheer would lift me out of my doldrums, and the world was made right.

W.C. attended the funeral, and soon reported that the clergyman, instead of celebrating Fred's accomplishments and what was strong and fine and gracious in Fred's life, chose to dwell on the evil of drink and how it had ruined the foolish man who had succumbed to it. The tone of Carl Jameson's voice over the phone told me how much he damned a clergyman who would do that to the memory of Fred, at his funeral.

That proved to be a season for grief. Barbara Puechner

had wrestled with illness for years. She had esophageal cancer, and the "cure" was to remove the affected portion of the esophagus and hang the stomach from what was left. The meant her normally horizontal stomach was now vertical, and that meant she had to take small amounts of food and then lie down so it could be digested. But the rearranged stomach put pressure on her heart, and she had been battling heart trouble with her usual wry humor. She loved to tell about the peculiar sensations and noises evoked by a stomach hanging from her throat, and thought it was the funniest thing ever to happen to her. She had moved to the California coast and was raising Glenna there when she died suddenly in Florida.

Then came still more bleak news. Sara Ann Freed, still in her fifties, had become mysteriously ill after surgery, and had suddenly died, the causes being something of a conundrum that the doctors could not answer. I reflected on that bright, sweet woman who had given my early career a hand-up, had faith in me, saw me through my first half-dozen novels, and was schooling me and improving my work all the while. Without her, I never would have become a novelist. She had come from a Mennonite background in rural Pennsylvania, climbed the ladder in New York, married her beloved Ira, and ended up a vice president of Warner Books and senior editor at Mysterious Press. She and Ira had a home in Manhattan, and the latchstring was out if ever I should come to New York. We had drifted apart, but every once in a while there she would be on the phone, and we would catch up. She had come to Montana, visited me in Big Timber, and still took a lively interest in the West. She and Ira seriously considered buying a second home in my town. And then she was gone, her life cut short.

In moments of great quietness I can hear the voices of the lost, and remember them with gratitude.

17

Experiments

IN SPITE OF MY DEEPENING PESSIMISM ABOUT THE
FUTURE OF WESTERN FICTION, I continued to
experiment with stories that might win readers
who were not familiar with the field, or had been
driven off by the usual gunman stories. I had thought
much about the virtues of the western hero. There are
many forms of courage, and I thought it might make
good reading to have a look at some of them. Western
heroes traditionally have physical courage. They stare
into the muzzles of guns. They deal with danger. They
face mobs. They face violence bravely and without
complaint. But what of all the other virtues that give
greatness to people? What about moral or ethical
courage? Could I create western heroes with that sort
of courage and resolve? And would they sell?

I drafted some proposals for novels built around

moral courage, and Robin Rue submitted them to Dan Slater, who edited the western line for New American Library. These were pretty radical for western fiction, and I wondered about their fate. In one story, a bank clerk in a small western town refuses to lie in court no matter what pressures were applied to him by his powerful employer. In the next story, a former stage coach robber who has lived quietly with his wife and family for years, becoming model citizens in a small Utah town, is plagued by conscience and decides to reveal his past and to make restitution to the victims of his robberies. He courageously begins to do that, only to find that his community doesn't like the idea one bit. And the third proposed novel was about a courageous woman newspaper editor in a Kansas cowtown who faces a cruel dilemma. Her own son, the mayor of the town, is utterly corrupt, and she decides to expose him in her paper because it is the right thing to do, no matter how much anguish it might cause her.

All three of these stories would focus on moral or ethical courage, not physical courage. All three would involve realistic dilemmas often faced by people in the West. All of these stories would be on turf that had scarcely been touched by the thousands of stories pumped out by western novelists over an entire century of western fiction. Indeed, my stories most closely resembled a few early western novels rather than the recent variety. One can go straight back to *The Virginian* and discover its hero wrestling with rights and wrongs at every juncture. Zane Grey's stories also wrestled with right and wrong. But not long after that, questions of right and wrong more or less vanished from western stories. I had high hopes that this series might help restore some of the readers who had drifted away when westerns grew more and more nihilistic.

Robin did a bang-up job presenting the proposals to Dan Slater, for next I knew he made a handsome offer on all three and we were in business. These stories excited me. Instead of merely hunting for new topics for my stories, I had moved to different tonal ground. My stories were about people with unbending rectitude in the face of truly sinister and life-threatening challenge. Slater wanted something to tie the novels together, so I created a narrator, a wise old postmaster who knew the characters, and prefaced the stories with his comments about what would follow.

I wrote these novels as if I had been liberated from the usual western forms. The hero of the first story, *The Witness*, endures every imaginable menace to himself and his family and his livelihood. He endures threats of imprisonment, and yet he is determined to tell the whole truth in court, and does so, at terrible cost. NAL gave it a good cover and published it. Some critics called it predictable, but it was a finalist for a Spur Award, and I was satisfied with it. The second one, which the publishers called *Restitution* against my wishes (too many syllables, and the sound of clacking teeth) was perhaps the most poignant, and offered some social commentary as well. The whole idea of a former robber and his wife trying to repay what had been taken from others many years earlier, had a certain fascination about it and I had a chance to probe what people really think about reformed criminals. It too received a fine cover, and was also a Spur Award finalist. The third of these stories, *Drum's Ring*, seemed to acquire a life of its own as I wrote it. I especially love writing when I can sit back and be an observer. Angie Drum, the widow who had inherited her husband's weekly cowtown paper, took on her own son's corrupt ring of politicians, not to mention a fearsome trail herd boss, and for her moral courage she came to grief. That one won a Spur Award, my fourth.

The three novels didn't do well for NAL, and at one point I apologized to Dan Slater. But he graciously reminded me that a three-book series that had produced a Spur winner and two finalists was as much as any author could achieve; I had given them some fine literature, and it was up to them to turn a profit on it. The series did do some good subsidiary rights business, and I hope that some day it will pan out for New American Library. I admire

Dan Slater and the company for taking a chance on some unusual fiction.

I soon had contracts for more original mass-market books at NAL, one of them a biographical novel about Wyatt Earp. My Masterson novel had been a success, so maybe it was time to try writing about another western icon. I was prepared for trouble. There are few people more contentious than Tombstone buffs. The gunfight at the OK Corral rivets half the screwballs in the country. The whole field is riddled with dubious sources, unproven assertions, and acrimony. There were Earp partisans and debunkers, but in recent years the debunkers had lost ground because a stream of new primary source material being unearthed in the eighties and nineties uniformly substantiated the Earp brothers' version of the events in Tombstone and the shootout near the OK Corral. Long ago I had supposed that researchers had reached a dead end and there would be little more uncovered about that legendary episode, but I was wrong. A Tombstone stringer named Clara Brown had been sending regular dispatches about events in the mining town to a San Diego paper, including detailed accounts of the Earps' troubles with the Cowboys. And what is now called the Forrestine Hooker manuscript was dug out of a museum in California where it has rested uncatalogued since the 1920s. It added valuable detail to the whole story. In the 1880s exchanges were the medium by which papers picked up news from other locales. Papers simply exchanged subscriptions and published the news that they garnered from the exchange papers. Researchers were uncovering material originally published in Tombstone that was reprinted in such places as San Diego, San Francisco, and Tucson, with the result that valuable material from Tombstone papers thought to be lost was found in the verbatim reprints. And without major exception, all of it supported the contentions of the Earp brothers. In addition to all that, two new and valuable studies of the Earps and Tombstone had been published, and added to the riches I had at hand. I feasted on all that and began writing.

I wanted to humanize Wyatt Earp, and remove him from the iconic image of a gunman, and see what sort of person he really was, what he was like with his wife, Josie, how he behaved with his brothers, what he really believed, and what people in Tombstone really thought of him. I wanted to puncture the mythology and get to the real man, the one who was a deacon in the Methodist Church in Dodge City. NAL changed my title, *Wyatt Earp's Story*, to the hoary *Trouble in Tombstone*, which had graced a few other covers over the years, but that was all right. The book did reasonably well, but any book about the Earps does well. It even garnered a little praise.

By the late 1990s it was plain that the fiction of the American West was fading. It looked more and more to me, at least, that this branch of American literature would be neatly confined to the 20th century. It had begun with Owen Wister's *The Virginian* in 1902 and might not last beyond the book's hundredth birthday in 2002. Candy Moulton, the editor of WWA's *Roundup* Magazine began a series celebrating the great western novelists of the 20th century, and also commissioned a piece about the centenary of Wister's great novel. All of this had a funereal quality. It was as if the organization devoted to western literature could only look backward because there was no future.

Few editors were attending the conventions, but Dan Slater and Tom Doherty faithfully made their appearances. The conventions were no longer a significant marketplace. There was a steady trickle of grim news from New York; western lines were either folding or being cut back. Trade magazines no longer covered western fiction and neglected to list awards won in that field. It was as if western fiction had vanished from the national consciousness. The younger generations had not seen a western film in a theater or read a western and scarcely knew such things existed.

There have been learned treatises written about the decline. These usually focus on modern urbanization or our increasing distance from the frontier. Some focus on the shift of values: westerns have real heroes but modern readers are more skeptical and cynical about human nature. All these theories have validity, and I wouldn't dispute them. I would employ Occam's Razor here and say that western fiction and movies simply went out of fashion, pushed aside and eventually forgotten. Fashion is both simple and mysterious. It shifts in unfathomable ways. It is far more deeply rooted in the past than people realize. It defies publicists. It is constantly demolishing icons. It celebrates new things and drives other things offstage. The literary field that had consumed my life is now utterly unfashionable. Most publishers try to ride fashion rather than defy it, and that meant abandoning western fiction and heading for "chic lit," or other trendy genres. There are well-known authors who have written superb books only to see them bomb because the world has moved mysteriously on to other authors with other stories to tell. In previous decades, when talking to the educated about literature, I had discovered contempt for western fiction; it was subliterature, it was racist and sexist, and so on. But by the late nineties even that was moot. Fashion had booted it out of our consciousness.

Over in the Western Literature Association, the academic organization supposedly devoted to the literature of the West, the consideration of traditional western fiction had largely vanished. One English professor of my acquaintance who wished to present a paper on the 1940s western novelist Ernest Haycox, found himself shuffled into the last slot on the schedule when most of the members had gone home, and read his paper to an audience of two or three. For several years I examined the WLA website to ascertain what these scholars were up to, and one thing was clear: they were no longer examining western literature. They had become sociologists absorbed with the social implications of the material they were examining. I took it as another sign that we had shifted into a new era, with new tastes. If fiction is examined at all at WLA conferences, it is examined for its social consequences, or as a reflection of the author's character.

A branch of literature never quite dies. It persists in niche markets. Occasionally there are brief revivals. A few titles are published by houses that pay substandard royalties. Dead authors are published more often than the living. All that is true of western fiction today. But it has virtually vanished from the national consciousness and I don't expect genre western fiction to return.

Even as commercial western fiction was fading, Western Writers of America was changing. The membership rolls burgeoned, easing the organization's chronic cash crunch. New members tended to write nonfiction and were often academics. Nonfiction writers now outnumbered the fiction writers. It seemed plain to me that the organization's future would lie in nonfiction, which was being published largely by university presses. WWA could survive even if western fiction vanished entirely. It was also plain to me, from reading the membership news in the magazine, that the bylaws were being interpreted liberally. *The Roundup* was looking just fine under the able editorship of Candy Moulton, and the amazing Doris Meredith was somehow reviewing twenty or thirty books per issue, offering intelligent comment on all those titles.

All of this evoked some long, hard looks at my own writing life. There I was, writing in a field that was almost daily withering away. I didn't much worry about the disappearance of genre westerns, the mass-market originals put into drugstore racks each month. They weren't about the West, and could just as well be set in West Virginia. They were about male warfare, and had almost nothing to do with the vast trans-Mississippi country that was scarcely known at the beginning of the 19th century. If those mass-market gunman lines, mistakenly called westerns by publishers and distributors, were to vanish overnight, there would be no harm done, and maybe novels of the real, historic, geographic West might flourish. Still, we live in a world of preconceptions, and few readers are able to sort out the differences between pocket books with gunmen on the covers, and stories of the real West. The decline of the mass-market lines was eroding interest in other writing about the West, especially historicals. There was trouble afoot. The question was how to deal with it. One possibility was to jump ship. I thought I could fashion a workable mystery, and I might try to pierce that crowded field. It would mean starting over. The readership I had acquired in my field would not carry over. But at bottom, the passion to write about the West as it really was, to tell the thousand stories that the thousands of genre westerns never told, is what gripped my imagination.

I decided to focus on biographical novels, which seemed almost exempt from the public perception of western literature. A novel about an historic figure seems to rise above category. I had already done a couple, focusing on two western lawmen, but there was no shortage of other absorbing people waiting in the wings. I chose Lewis and Clark as my first subjects, and began researching them.

Meanwhile, I continued with existing contracts. *The Fields of Eden*, for Forge, was another large, hardcover historical novel, this one about the settlement of Oregon. I had a chance to portray one of my heros, Dr. John McLoughlin, the magnificent chief factor of Hudson's Bay Company at Fort Vancouver, who dominated the territory disputed by England and the United States. And I was continuing with my Skye's West novels, writing *Dark Passage*, and *Going Home*.

Dark Passage received some truly marvelous notices, such as these:

> Richard Wheeler's latest Barnaby Skye saga is more than just an entertaining frontier adventure. It is a love story told in terms as ruggedly beautiful as the mountain country in which it is set. . . . A Western Writers of America Golden Spur winner, Wheeler has a sharp eye for detail and writes prose worth savoring.
>
> —*Booklist*

I approached reviewing. . . .*Dark Passage* with a large
degree of trepidation. I started simultaneously reading
the new Anne Rice novel, *The Vampire Armand*, thinking
it would eventually capture my imagination, and I would
then return Wheeler's book to my editor, telling him I just
couldn't make a connection with it . . . . But instead, in
the war of words, Richard Wheeler kicked Anne Rice's pre-
tentious butt. All of the details and characters ring true.
Wheeler is especially adept at inventing believable Indian
characters. The pacing of the novel is impeccable. He
blends various white and Indian cultures together into a
believable world with never a false beat. *Dark Passage* is
well worth reading.

—*The Missoulian*

The bicentennial of the Lewis and Clark Expedition was
approaching, and I thought to write a timely book that would take
advantage of the publicity surrounding that great event. As usual,
Robin Rue landed a contract for me. I would have time to finish
and publish the book a year or so ahead of the rush of histories and
novels I knew would accompany that celebration. There was an
abundant literature, and I gradually worked through some of it. I
was fascinated not only by the expedition, but also by Meriwether
Lewis's astonishing decline after he returned, which culminated
in his death, possibly by suicide, only three years later. What had
caused it? Why was Lewis so sick? Why had his judgment failed
him? Why had he been unable to edit the expedition journals and
have them published?

It dawned on me that perhaps that was what this novel
should be about. There would be plenty of other authors writing
about the three-year trip, but I doubted that anyone would pick
up the story of Lewis and Clark after they returned.

One day, in Billings, I was conversing with Bill Walton, a
doctor who lectured on the medicines of the expedition, and I

asked him if he had any idea what had destroyed Lewis so swiftly upon his return, just when he should have been on top of the world. Was it malaria? I asked.

It might have been, Walton replied. Lewis had come from the Virginia Piedmont where malaria was endemic. But it was more likely that Lewis had syphilis.

I suddenly realized I had a novel. But my friend couldn't recollect where he had come across that diagnosis. I returned to my research and began to hunt for it, working through everything I could find about Lewis, checking footnotes, studying bibliographies. And then, in a monograph about Lewis's rather twisted character, I found what I was looking for. The thesis that Lewis was suffering from syphilis and that his death by suicide might well be ascribed to his depression about his disease had been advanced by a Seattle physician and epidemiologist named Reimert Thorolf Ravenholt. I was able to download his Lewis papers, and my novel was born that very hour.

18

All About People

DOCTOR RAVENHOLT'S SHREWD DETECTIVE WORK HAD UNCOVERED THE STORY IN THE EXPEDITION'S JOURNALS. The entries only hinted at what happened but nonetheless the evidence was there, not only in entries themselves, but also in the dates of the entries noting the onset of illnesses. Just as telling were Meriwether Lewis's account ledgers that he faithfully kept upon his return; especially his payments to a St. Louis physician known for his skills in dealing with venereal diseases. Lewis had contracted syphilis from the Shoshones. Right on schedule, the primary syphilis gravely affected him as he traveled along the Snake River, a period when he was so sick that Clark kept the journals and took over the command. Eventually, Lewis's disease turned into the dreaded neurosyphilis, the form of the disease that affects the nervous system and brain, resulting in bad judgment, bouts of emotion, and mental debility.

What about a novel that moved from Lewis's triumph upon his return, when he and Clark became the darlings of the young republic and Thomas Jefferson bestowed honors on them, to his death on the Natchez Trace three years later? Would the theme be too gloomy? I decided to tackle it. The gloominess would be relieved by William Clark's marriage and success. In fact, the opposing fates of the two explorers would provide good story contrast. I also thought the theme would attract attention and my novel would be perused widely. Little did I know at that point that there is a whole Lewis and Clark Establishment devoted to polishing the escutcheons of the explorers, and that my novel would be carefully buried by those people and would not appear in a single bibliography or reading list that would be prepared for the three-year bicentennial celebration. And the one review from an Establishment journal would be dour. Yet, an odd thing happened. By the end of the bicentennial, I noted that commentators were taking Lewis's syphilis for granted.

It was an exciting and challenging project, and I tackled it with both dread and determination. Some historians believed Lewis suffered from malaria, then known as ague, and Lewis may have thought so also. In the novel I have him using malaria as his public explanation for chronic illness. The governor of Upper Louisiana could suffer ague without raising eyebrows; he could not reveal the true nature of his affliction, and when his syphilis could no longer be concealed, he knew he had but one option, which he exercised with his brace of pistols on the Natchez Trace. It would be a tragic novel, a man fighting a tragic fate that would not only debilitate him, but shame a national hero.

Life in those millennial years was good. Sue and I had worked out a modus vivendi. Her teaching schedule and other commitments enabled her to come to Livingston only every four or five weeks, but we made the best of those moments. She usually arrived on Friday and returned to Billings on Sunday. Each meeting was a rendezvous. We hosted dinners, and she made my friends her own. We maintained an active social life. In turn, I traveled to Billings fairly often, met and enjoyed her friends, and partook of her life there. We saw each other perhaps three weekends a month. When people asked us what a long-distance marriage was like, we told them it was like a honeymoon. The commuting was easy: we sailed along an uncrowded Interstate winding through the Yellowstone River valley, one and three-quarters hours from door to door. That was less than many commutes in and out of big cities. Soon we were attending conferences together, including the new Montana Book Festival in Missoula as well as my Western Writers of America conventions. In 2000 we drove to Kerrville, Texas, and in 2001, to Idaho Falls, Idaho. Sue is an aficionado of the literature of the West, though not its genre fiction, and she happily fell in with the writers I counted among my closest friends. She had written several pieces about Dorothy M. Johnson for WWA's *Roundup Quarterly*, and was known to some members even before she first arrived on my arm, so to speak.

Her PBS documentary about Johnson was floundering on financial shoals, and years slid by without much progress. I thought perhaps WWA might help fund this study of one of its most illustrious members, whose short stories had been turned into major films: *The Man Who Shot Liberty Valance*, starring John Wayne, James Stewart, and Lee Marvin; *The Hanging Tree*, starring Gary Cooper and Maria Schell; and *A Man Called Horse*, starring Richard Harris and Dame Judith Anderson.

We invited my neighbor Margot Kidder over and Sue persuaded her to become the voice of Dorothy Johnson. She had also lined up Stan Lynde, the able cartoonist and novelist of the West, to narrate the documentary. Later I watched Kidder as she worked in the PBS studio on the Bozeman campus, and marveled at her gifts of interpretation. Stan Lynde was an old friend of Dorothy Johnson, and caught every nuance with grace. Sue and her crew had filmed Don Coldsmith, Bill Gulick, and Elmer Kelton, who had anecdotes or assessments to offer. We sent the presentation tape and a cover letter seeking funding for the project to Loren Estleman, the president of WWA at that time, but he never responded. The documentary languished for another year and a half, until a new president, Paul Andrew Hutton, and a new board, were in place. Hutton is an able historian actively involved with TV documentaries and is a talking head on the History Channel. The prospects seemed better, so Sue once again approached WWA's executive board, and this time received funding enough to finish up the project, something for which she and I are profoundly grateful. It was released on Montana PBS in 2005 to much acclaim, and was a finalist for a Spur Award. The administrator of the Johnson estate was so delighted with it that she made a large contribution to Montana PBS. No husband was ever so proud of his wife.

But I am ahead of my story. In the late nineties the Pinnacle license for my *Rocky Mountain Company* series was about to expire, and I applied for a reversion. I didn't know whether I could resell the series but I wanted the rights returned to me. It was written while I was sick and hadn't done well. None of the three novels earned out its modest advance. But I have always sought reversions when publishers were done with a book. To my astonishment, Pinnacle's attorney wrote back to say the company would put the three back into print. They put superb new covers on all three, evocative of the West, with endless western skies, buffalo, and wilderness trading posts. I was so delighted with these that I wrote the company thanking them. They seemed a little astonished: publishers are far more familiar with writers who are bitching about covers. The books were reissued and did well, paying off the advances and earning me substantial sums for several years. So the novels that were torn out of me when I was so sick with Epstein-Barr were adding substantially to my income more than a decade later. They are still bringing in a trickle of cash. I was impressed with Pinnacle. These weren't the usual gunfighter covers, but powerful evocations of the unsettled West, and they worked. They sold a lot of books.

That sweet year, 2001, was a banner one for me. For starters, I was enjoying a perpetual honeymoon. One day a call came that changed my life. Dale Walker told me that I would be the next Owen Wister Award recipient and would receive my bronze buffalo at the Idaho convention. It came out of the blue. I had not considered myself a candidate. I had started writing fiction late in life and believed I would not qualify for any award for lifetime achievement. In any case, I was still in my sixties and I knew there was a queue of older men and women who deserved the honor. On the few occasions I had ever wondered about receiving the award, I supposed that I might be a candidate in a decade or so. But there it was.

Dale Walker followed through with a splendid biographical article in *The Roundup* magazine. Biography is his natural gift, and I marveled at his grasp of my work and life. Part of his questioning me about my life helped me come to grips with my early failure as a newsman, which was something I hadn't talked about because it embarrassed me. But suddenly I was able to talk freely of my early life. He even rounded up affectionate observations from friends and colleagues, which moved me. One, from Loren Estleman, likening me to Conrad Richter, seemed to me an affirmation of all that I had struggled to achieve. There were others from Win Blevins, Elmer Kelton, Robin Rue and several more colleagues. I read all that not quite believing, as if they were speaking of someone, anyone, else.

To this day I do not know who was on that Wister committee, so I thanked all the usual suspects and hoped I had reached the right parties. The Spur Awards Banquet at the Shilo Inn was memorable. I hardly knew what to say in my acceptance speech, so I thought to give my friends and colleagues a word of encouragement. There were, I said, potential Willa Cathers and Ernest Hemingways and John Steinbecks sitting right there in that ballroom, and it was my belief that they would flourish in their chosen vocation. I believed it deeply. Over the years I had discovered a fabulous pool of talent in WWA, largely unnoticed because we were all writing unfashionable literature.

The next astonishment was that Tom Doherty sprang up, asked to speak for a few moments, and I found myself listening to an affectionate history of my long association with Tor and Forge, and his pride in publishing me. Again I was moved. They had taken their chances on me when I was little known. I have been blessed with a great primary publisher. When I reached my table, where my wife and her children had gathered, I received a loving hug from Sue.

Later that year, the phone rang and it was my former editor Harriet MacDougal, which astonished me because we hadn't been in touch for some while. Had I seen the current *Publishers Weekly*? Had I seen the starred lead review of my Skye's West novel, *Downriver*? I hadn't. She mailed it to me. It is framed and on my office wall. I was surprised. I had never imagined that one of my series novels would receive a starred review, much less a lead review.

Here is what PW said:

> Wheeler's westerns just keep getting better and better. . . . This is the best of the Skye novels so far, an adventure mystery full of suspense, action, historical color and careful portrayals of men and women facing hard choices amid uncertainty and danger. Wheeler is a master of character and plot, and this novel showcases his talents at their peak.

I had received all that a person writing in an unfashionable branch of American literature could hope for. Unless I was Larry McMurtry, I would not be reviewed in *The New York Times* or the *Washington Post* or other major literary venues. That was all right. The literature of the West appealed mostly to westerners, and would be little understood in Manhattan. They would sooner review some clichéd "chic lit" than review a western. In those heady times, as a way of keeping my feet on the ground, I occasionally reminded myself that none of my novels were on anyone's all-time best western list. Every five years or so, a jury of western writers assesses the all-time best novels, short stories, nonfiction, and films for *The Roundup,* and nothing of mine ever made the cut. I continued to think of myself as a middling kind of guy, writing middling-quality stories.

Sue and her PBS colleagues, armed with an infusion from the western writers organization, set to work finishing the documentary. In an archive at the Mansfield Library in Missoula, they and the librarians working with them found an entire uncatalogued box of Johnson photos, which solved one of their remaining problems, which was that they were short of visuals. Sue was able to help the university librarians identify people with Johnson in those photos, so there was a happy quid pro quo. Now, at last, Sue could write her script, they could have Margot Kidder and Stan Lynde do the narratives, and they could begin to assemble and edit a polished documentary. Even so, it would be years before the documentary would be aired, mostly because obtaining rights to quote or read anything of Johnson's proved to be time-consuming and complex. It took Macintosh and Otis, the unenthusiastic literary agents handling Johnson's estate, many months to grant permissions.

I returned to my writing, focusing on the biographies now. I had several in mind, including Thomas Francis Meagher, the acting governor of Montana who vanished from a Fort Benton riverboat, Major Marcus Reno, the scapegoat of the Custer battle, and Buffalo Bill Cody. Robin Rue obtained excellent contracts for all of these, plus more Skye's West stories. But Forge was experiencing the same economic trends that had forced so many other publishers to abandon or radically shrink their output of western material, and the completion deadlines for these new Forge projects stretched far into the future. Word sifted down that the company would reduce its western output, hanging on to only a few of its writers. And it was also pushing publication dates as far into the future as the contracts permitted. In short, western fiction was not doing the company's bottom line much good. Once again I was dealing with giant forces beyond my control.

I still needed to earn a living, though I was past the usual retirement age. I had salted away all I could in an IRA and other investments, but it would not be enough to support me should I lose my publishing income. I calculated that if I could stay fully employed through age seventy-five, I might be able to relax a little after that if inflation or bad investments didn't ruin my plans. That was the price I was paying for a bad start. I had no vested pension awaiting me.

It was time to try something else: My biographical novels were stretched so far into the future I would have time enough to write some traditional westerns. I proposed a series of frontier mining novels and Robin Rue placed the proposal before Ann LaFarge at Pinnacle. She liked the deal, and contracted for three. The five-grand advances weren't much, but they would keep me afloat. And I would have some fun walking in Bret Harte's shoes.

19

Controversies

BACK IN THE NINETIES, I WROTE A PIECE IN *THE ROUNDUP* CALLED "GRACE UNDER PRESSURE: A Beleaguered Literary Genre," in which I examined some of the accusations being laid at the doorstep of western fiction, such as that westerns are racist, sexist, and imperialist. Western fiction was not lacking its critics. These include John G. Cawelti, Richard Slotkin, Leslie Fiedler, Richard Etulain and William Kittredge.

Some of these authors used a few examples to buttress their case, especially Slotkin. Others tended merely to opinionize. But over most of a century, many thousands of westerns had been published, and these varied sharply from decade to decade, and it was plain that the critics had scarcely sampled this vast array of literature and were drawing conclusions that had no solid basis in research.

These people, armed with a few exemplars, were generalizing about a whole branch of American literature, and I didn't think they were on solid ground.

I wrote that "no disciplined, scholarly, unbiased research dealing broadly with the values, themes, ideals, plots and characters in westerns, decade by decade from 1900 to the present, has ever been done."

Much to my astonishment one day I received a call from an old WWA friend, Jeffrey Wallmann, and learned he was pursuing his doctoral degree at the University of Nevada, and would be taking up my challenge. He was doing an in-depth study of the fiction of the frontier and the West from its origins to the present. He said he got the idea from reading my article. Later, he shared the draft with me, and asked me to write a foreword, which was most flattering.

In his own introductory chapter, he said my proposal was impossible to fulfill; there was simply too much ground to be covered. Nonetheless, Wallmann had systematically read over six hundred western stories drawn from the entire period, and was able to reach some well-grounded conclusions. The amount of reading that Wallmann did was simply staggering. The result was a dissertation, published by Texas Tech University Press, which is easily the most sophisticated and comprehensive study of the genre ever done.

What Wallmann discovered from all that research was that most westerns were simply stories without any ideological freight, and these often reflected the values of the period in which they were written. The nature of the stories tended to change with the contemporary social values of the times.

"What Jeffrey Wallmann had done in this remarkable study," I wrote in the foreword, "is show how complex the genre really is, and how difficult it is to categorize the literature of the westward expansion in any simplistic way . . . . As would be expected, he has found that *none* of the clichés casually assumed by academics and critics is valid."

I also wrote that Wallmann's researches revealed that westerns "expressed no particular values at all other than those common to all literature, such as hope, or courage, or faith in the future. The stories were expressions of their times, and the authors who wrote them were simply writing according to their lights . . . ."

Wallmann's study concludes on an optimistic note: "In America, especially during the last forty years, no field of literature has acted more responsibly as a means of making us see ourselves, and in years to come western fiction will create a new mythology, or rather, a revision of the frontier myth that will reflect—as westerns always do—prevailing cultural beliefs, goals, and dreams. It will be told in a modern narrative blend which employs more realism, yet keeps to the tradition of relating frontier adventures about personal character striving to overcome perilous circumstances. And all the while the western will be making meaning, will be as current as tomorrow's newspaper."

Fashion seems to be dictating otherwise. And the doyens of political correctness in academia are not inclined to exonerate a genre they have condemned, no matter that Jeff Wallmann's work should give them pause. It seems best simply to acknowledge that genre western fiction has been driven offstage and is not likely to return.

But I have always felt that there are other ways to depict the westward expansion, and biography is one of them. Biography is mainstream. I turned to Thomas Francis Meagher, one of the most astonishing characters ever to wander into the American West, and also one of the most controversial. Meagher grew up in Waterford, Ireland, in comfortable circumstances. But the starvation conditions of 1840s Ireland and the oppressions of the British radicalized him, and he soon was one of the leading separatists, advocating Irish independence and the freedom of Catholics to practice their faith unhindered. His attempts to stir up a peasant uprising were laughable, and he was tried and sentenced to be hanged, drawn and quartered by Queen Victoria's magistrates. An international uproar saved Meagher's life and he was transported to Tasmania in permanent exile.

With the help of American Irish, he escaped, reached New York, practiced law, married a rich American woman, Libby Townsend, and dabbled in get-rich-quick schemes. When the Civil War broke out he organized the Irish Brigade, which fought valiantly on the Union side and may have rescued the Army of the Potomac from disaster on more than one occasion. But Brigadier General Meagher was a gabby drinker, got into trouble several times, and eventually was cashiered shortly before Appomattox, probably for being a soak. President Andrew Johnson took pity on him and made him secretary of the new Territory of Montana, which was the equivalent of being lieutenant governor. No sooner did Meagher arrive at the gold camp of Bannack than Governor Sidney Edgerton handed him the government seals and fled to Washington. The Acting Governor, as Meagher called himself, soon got into trouble with almost everyone, was threatened by the local vigilantes, and eventually vanished from a riverboat docked at Fort Benton. Montanans have been arguing ever since whether it was murder, sickness, or booze that did in Meagher. There are good arguments on all sides.

There is a body of literature about Meagher's life in Ireland, but I decided not to tackle it in detail; this would be a novel about Meagher in America. I began the story with his escape from the penal colony and his arrival in New York. I found myself liking Meagher even though opinion about him is as polarized as it is about other major western figures. He was earnest, likeable, bright, and loquacious, even eloquent. But his gift of words was no weapon at all against malevolent men bristling with schemes and politics and guns, who made short work of him in letters sent to the powerful

Republicans who dominated the postwar congress and were trampling on the South just as hard as they could. Meagher, a Union man, was accused of supporting the South, which was nonsense. Things came to a head in 1867, when he went to Fort Benton to pick up rifles sent upriver by the army, and vanished.

I thought that made a good ending to the story. What better than to leave readers wondering? A lot of canny research has been done about that disappearance, and there is a large body of material, all of it contradictory. A retired FBI man of my acquaintance who applied his forensic skills to the available evidence concluded Meagher had been murdered. More conservative historians think he was sick and fell into the river and drowned. Others think he was drunk and fell into the drink. Still others think maybe the radical Irish Fenians, whom he had offended, put one of their own to death. The body was never found. It is all fodder for conspiracy theorists.

I have no idea what happened in Fort Benton. I can make a case for any one of the possibilities. That was the very stuff of good storytelling, and eventually I completed my third biographical novel, *The Exile*. It most certainly was not a western, and its cover featured a civil war battle scene involving the Irish Brigade. The book was only lightly reviewed, perhaps because my name is associated with the literature of the West, and I was out of my usual pigeonhole. I was reminded that people who make a name in one literary venue rarely escape it. A couple of Meagher relatives have announced their approval of the novel. The last time I was in Virginia City, Montana, where Meagher's cottage still stands, and where he governed, the local bookseller had never heard of my novel. But it continues to be in print, and sells a few copies not to western buffs, but to the Irish, for Meagher is one of the great heros of Hibernia.

I was ready to tackle another biography, and who better than Buffalo Bill Cody? There was a substantial literature about him, almost all of it agreeing that he was a superb scout for the army during the Indian wars, but conflicted about the rest of his life. Was he a great showman, or merely a puppet propped up in the arenas by the skilled entrepreneurs who were his business partners? There were hecklers and hagiographers. The man looked like a Greek god, but was his head full of sawdust? He was trapped in arguably one of the worst marriages ever made, but that only made his life more absorbing for a biographer. He was surrounded by talent, notably Annie Oakley, and there was a solid literature about her as well. I had no preconceived opinions about the man, and plunged in to the research looking for a lead, a hook, a way to tell the story.

I arrived at a startling and radical idea. I would begin the novel with his death at the beginning of 1917, and then let his friends, family, associates, enemies, and partners reminisce about him. In that way I could express a variety of opinions. The worrisome aspect of such a plan was that it didn't directly narrate a story. There would be no narrative thread leading from one event in Cody's life to another. What there would be was conflict. I added a fictional posthumous memoir from Cody to give him a say in what would be a free-for-all recapitulation of his colorful life. I broached all this to my editor, Dale Walker, but I sensed he didn't much like the idea. Each chapter was labeled, and was a first-person reminiscence. Thus I could move, chapter by chapter, from his wife Louisa to Annie Oakley to his partner Pawnee Bill, and so on. I particularly enjoyed working with the Annie Oakley segments, because I had a good idea, never before explored, about what finally drove them apart and why she left the show when it was playing in England. I visited the Buffalo Bill Historical Center in Cody, where his memorabilia are on display and there are experts at hand, including Dr. Paul Fees, who gave me a bibliography to work with. The museum's vast Cody exhibit is, if anything, timid and didn't hint of the controversies surrounding the man and in fact did its best to conceal them.

Eventually I completed the novel and sent it along to Dale

Walker. He had it a long time, and when it came back, I saw his green pen had been busy. In short, he didn't like it at all, felt it was largely repetition, and devoid of motion. He had cut most of it, requested revision of much of the rest, but his notes indicated that he really wanted me to start over. The thing just plain didn't work. He hoped I could salvage some of the material and put it into a straight narrative of Cody's life, in chronological order, told by Cody himself, or perhaps a single narrator. I read over the notes and realized he was right. It didn't work. It was repetitive. I was in considerable anguish because I simply didn't know what to do, or how to start over. I didn't doubt that Walker had spared me, and Forge, a great embarrassment. In fact, it was a mark of Walker's courage that he could come to those conclusions and gracefully inform his old friend and colleague that the story didn't work.

That was painful news. A lot of labor had gone into it, and now it was lost. Maybe I was getting old. I finally realized I had to shelve it. I could not find any way to make a novel out of it. I wrote him, saying I was shelving the story. He had hoped I'd start anew, but I couldn't find a way to do it. So the Cody novel remained on a shelf for a year and a half while I undertook other projects. I arranged with Forge to convert the Cody contract into another Skye's West novel.

But this story had a happy ending. One day a long time later, I pulled the Cody novel out of its casket and began reading. It was repetitive, all right. But the more I read, the more I grasped a way out of the problem. You can have several observers describing the same event if they all have conflicting views of it or intriguing insights missed by the others. I could rewrite the novel and maintain its radical form so long as all those reminiscences were sharply at odds and diverse. But first I would need to cut. I took large chunks out of the story, maybe twenty thousand words, and then examined what was left. It was a core that could be expanded with conflicting viewpoints about Cody, which would provide the necessary tension and the motion the novel would require. I had room in my schedule, and set to work, this time letting Cody and his family and his associates duke it out. It wasn't easy. When I had finished the new draft, I felt there still was some repetition, and I found ways of dealing with it. By trial and error I reached the point where I felt the novel was attractive and publishable, but I knew I had no publisher and might have trouble finding one.

I approached Sunstone Press, a Santa Fe regional publisher with a fine reputation, and its publisher, James Clois Smith, Jr., was soon sending a contract. All of this was a valuable experience for me. I had never before turned a failed novel into something viable. It remains a radical approach and there may be readers who are disappointed it is not simply a straight narrative of Cody's life. But the life is there, argued about, celebrated, condemned, by all those characters who knew the old showman. At this writing I don't know what its fate will be. Maybe it is the work of an addled old author. But if I succeeded, it will be acknowledged as a look into the heart of a very public man whose polished veneer hid his real self from the world.

Through that period I was writing my frontier mining camp stories for Pinnacle, and having fun. The first, which they titled *The Bounty Trail,* had a confidence man and charlatan named Colonel Claudius P. Raines for a central character. He and his doxy conspire to bring an abandoned mining town back to life by salting its closed mines. The second, which the publisher named *Vengeance Valley,* is about the discovery of bonanza gold squarely under a hospital owned by the Sisters of Charity in a ridge-top mining town, and the schemes to oust the nuns from their land. Its hero is a bashful prospector named Yancy who discovers the bonanza and tells the sisters about it. Its heroine is the senior nun running the hospital. The story was neither about vengeance nor did it take place in a valley. The third, which they named *Seven Miles to Sundown,* is about a lost gold mine supposedly near a New Mexico mining town called Rio Blanco. I rewrote the story to fit the title they gave it. Its hero is a lexicographer hunting new words in the wild west. He wears a deerstalker hat and knickers and is something of a laughingstock until he proves himself a much better man than the schemers looking for the lost mine.

I looked forward to the same sort of great covers that Pinnacle had put on my Rocky Mountain Company series, but it was not to be. They all featured the usual cowboys with guns blazing away. I rather wished they had strapped six-guns on my heroine nun, and had her blazing away, too. That might even have sold a book or two. Eventually I contracted for two more of those mining stories, this time from Gary Goldstein, who had replaced Ann LaFarge. Those mining stories also had cowboys with blazing guns on the covers, even though one of the heroes was a rat catcher working for a detective agency, and the other was a mining geologist who wore baggy tweeds and a pith helmet. All these cover paintings are of the sort churned out by freelance artists and purchased cheaply by the mass-market houses and slapped onto westerns without regard to the content. The same unconcern is true of the titles, which usually evoke old western novels and are intended to sound familiar. *Vengeance Valley* had been used on several novels in the past.

The problem here is that all these gunman covers were deceptive. They were touting a type of ranch story that didn't exist between the covers. To be sure, they were instantly identifiable as westerns, but there were no cowboys in any of my stories, and the heroes were in mining vocations. Few of these stories involved blazing guns or shootouts. The cover copy didn't help much, either, but was usually a bit more accurate than the art. The people who bought my novels discovered that my stories had nothing to do with the covers. This has been a commonplace practice among mass-market western lines for generations, and continues even now. And one by one, readers who discover that the covers don't even remotely depict the book's contents, simply give up on westerns. They've been hoodwinked too many times, and turn to more reliable literature.

I don't know why book packagers do that, and why they pick on the western lines. It's as if they want to *conceal* what's in the western stories rather than sell a novel on its merits. The practice insults the customers and supposes they are too dumb to care if they've been euchred. Economics is part of it. Those cowboy-with-a-gun cover paintings are scooped up from itinerant artists for very little. One of the reasons I feel lucky to be with Forge is that its covers are commissioned to depict the story, which costs more but pays off in the long run. One can always trust a Forge jacket or mass-market cover.

The practice is not confined to western lines but is most prevalent in them, and I believe it is one of several reasons why mass-market westerns have almost vanished. Perhaps I am too hard on these packaging and sales people who simply want to sell books, but my opinions are based on three decades of dealing with western fiction. If I am angry, it is not so much because this is bad marketing, but because what they are doing is wrong. The humblest book, even a *western*, deserves an honest cover that sells the book on its merits. A deceptive cover betrays the public, betrays the author, and betrays American literature.

The misnamed *Vengeance Valley*, about the shy prospector and the nuns, won a Spur Award, my fifth. Gary Goldstein flew out to the Spokane convention to share the moment, and I enjoyed seeing him.

20

In the Trenches

One thing about biographical novels: I had virtually no competition. There are very few novels written about real people. I don't know why. But these novels turned out to be a natural form for me, and evoked the best in me. One day I drove over to the Little Big Horn Battlefield to research my next novel, which would again deal with one of the mythic stories of the West. The Custer battle has been done to death in fiction, and there is a huge literature associated with it. But I had something a little different in mind: a novel about the scapegoat of the Little Big Horn, Major Marcus Reno.

Shortly after the battle he was widely celebrated as a hero who saved around half of the Seventh Cavalry from Custer's fate. But there were those who thought he had betrayed Custer, either by cowardice or by design. If he and the other officer commanding a column, Captain Frederick Benteen, had gone to Custer's aid, so this reasoning goes, Custer and his men would not have been exterminated. It's a nice theory. And it's always pleasant to have a scapegoat. You always want someone to blame for a disaster, and there are plenty of people who figure Marcus Reno failed his commanding officer one way or another.

I did not go into this project with a scholar's neutrality or objectivity. I was going to write a sympathetic novel about Marcus Reno, no matter that he was an unpleasant and unlikeable man, and I knew I would have a tough time making an unsympathetic man my protagonist. Reno was in trouble all his life and alienated those who might have helped him. He had barely scraped through West Point and was at the bottom of his class. His Civil War record was solid, and he received commendations. But after the war he lurched from one disaster to another, and was finally booted out of the army.

That sour nature may have been what has inspired numerous students of the battle to blame Reno above all, and to accuse him of deliberately permitting Custer and his five companies to be destroyed by refusing to ride to the rescue. That sort of thinking, which is grounded on the knowledge we now have of the disaster, rather than what was known to the command before it started the fight, is a classic paranoid construct and I suspect that the authors of such finger-pointing treatises are the same sort who believe that the CIA paid Lee Harvey Oswald to kill President Kennedy. There are always conspiracy theorists around doing their worst, and Marcus Reno was the victim of one of the most pernicious of those, a dime novelist named Captain Frederick Whittaker, who set out to ruin Reno, in cahoots with Elizabeth Custer. (Whittaker was so absorbed in his fantasies that he carried a revolver around his house to defend himself against lurking enemies, but one day his cane caught in the bannister, he tumbled down the stairs, and accidentally shot himself through the head. That was the fruit of his obsessions.)

In one sense, Reno's enemies failed. He was never convicted or condemned for his conduct during the battle. But in a larger sense, they succeeded. The gossip, malice, backbiting and finger-pointing took their toll on a man who was already unstable, and ruined him. My novel became the story of Marcus Reno's decline, somewhat like my novel of Meriwether Lewis's decline. I found ways to make Reno empathetic. My readings had revealed to me that he was at his best during his brief marriage to Mary Hannah Ross. He was stable and successful during those periods, and also well liked. But before and after the marriage, which ended with her early death, he reverted to his undisciplined conduct. He was one of those men who needed a woman to complete himself and keep him balanced.

I found the story of Reno's decline compelling, and tried to portray him as a man under pressure, without the inner resources to deal with the slanders circulating behind his back. He failed, of course, and spent the last decades of his life as a clerk in Washington, D.C. He also spent his entire competence on legal and political efforts to reinstate himself in the army. It never happened. He died of complications following cancer surgery at a young age. It wasn't until the 1960s that an army board granted him an honorable discharge which allowed him to be buried at the Custer Battlefield Cemetery, where he is the highest ranking officer.

I have a picture of myself at Reno's grave, taken by my friend Bill Lane. That grave always is decorated with real or artificial flowers. I suppose the descendants of some of those soldiers who survived the battle honor his resting place. I told Reno's spirit, in that windswept cemetery with its orderly white headstones, that I had tried to do him justice. I told him I hoped he had found the peace which eluded him during his restless days on earth.

I didn't know what the verdict would be about my novel. Contention about the Custer Battle far transcends and dwarfs all other contention in the history of the West, including the controversies about Billy the Kid, the Earp brothers, the innocence or guilt of Sheriff Plummer of Virginia City, Montana. There are people obsessed with that battle, people who ride horseback trying to replicate the lines of attack, and walk the bloodstained fields with stopwatches. There are people who amass the entire literature and try to sift and winnow the truth out of it. They profess to be objective. They are all going to let the facts speak for themselves. They say they will not draw unwarranted conclusions. They will set aside their prejudices. If new information warrants that they abandon their dearly-held views, they say they would find the courage to do it. But in the end, their biases leak out, and one can tell early on, when reading them, what direction they are heading. Their attitude toward Custer is always a bellwether. I believe few, if any, students of the battle began their studies in utter neutrality. That is because George Armstrong Custer's very nature invites scorn or admiration, awe or disgust. I do not know of any neutral commentators, though plenty will say they are. I was not neutral and I knew where I was going with the story even before I cracked open the first of my research volumes.

Because of the ferocity of opinion about the battle, I anticipated finding myself thoroughly roasted, especially by the Custerphiles. But when the book was published, that didn't happen. It was mostly ignored by history buffs because it was a novel, but it was also treated amiably, which astonished me.

Publishers Weekly had this to say about it:

> Although some might call this revisionist history, it is also compelling fiction, a fresh, insightful and compassionate tale of a tragic figure.

Forge, as usual, had put a handsome cover on it, which I am certain helped the mass-market sales. I am finding it rewarding to create an affectionate portrait of people who, for one reason or another, have damaged reputations. A novelist is free to go where historians may not go, into the realm of speculation or intuition, and if this is carefully done a novelist may plausibly enlarge the public's perception of a historic figure, or draw attention to the pressures and forces operating upon the subject of the novel. History is harsh and judgmental, and rarely explores the inner dynamics of people, their past, their diseases, their tragedies, their triumphs, all of which influence their conduct. That is the special realm and perhaps the gift of a biographical novelist, to convey the grace under pressure, or lack of it, in their subjects. At bottom, the novelist turns the harsh judgments of historians into tragedy. The novelist enables readers to see what joys and cruelties and ordeals life had visited upon the subject, and what emerges is not judgment but empathy. The novelist who deals with real people instills the tragic sense into the story, and this natural mission completes our understandings of historic figures. If I have done nothing else worthwhile in my work, I have at least humanized the subjects of my biographical novels.

As the publishing world changed, I found I could change with it. I am now in fields far removed from what I was writing when I started. My views have changed as well. I remember how angry I was in 1990 when the doyen of Montana literature, Professor William Kittredge, joyously proclaimed that regional authors "were finally getting out from beneath the western." I thought his observation smacked of snobbery. But now, as I write this in 2006, I utterly agree with Kittredge. Anyone who wants to write seriously about the American West needs to get out from under the western. Kittredge was simply seeing what I was not yet ready to see. I have gradually come to the conclusion that the decline of western fiction may be a good thing; it was suffocating the regional writing that counts. There will be better and truer stories of the West emerging just as soon as the whole ritualized and rickety ritual of the old western novel tumbles into the dust.

There was change afoot in Western Writers of America. The new faces I saw at conventions were younger and younger, which was to be expected. I was approaching my seventies. Everyone looks young to me now. But what I hadn't expected was the doubling of the membership to six hundred, in the space of a few years. This doubling had occurred during the period when sales of western fiction had declined, contracts were scarce, and several western lines had folded. It seemed a paradox. One day, from curiosity, I systematically perused the membership columns in WWA's magazine, *The Roundup*, over a five-year span, taking notes as I reviewed the material. I found the answers readily discernible. The membership committee was steadily admitting people who were not qualified. The casually-written membership news was an imperfect mirror of reality, but even so I was able to ascertain that a quarter to a third of the people entering WWA had few, if any, professional credits. I added up those members who I knew were still making a living or most of a living from writing western fiction or nonfiction, and they came to only a handful.

Publishing was changing precipitously, and so was the western writing organization. Ever since a few giant conglomerates had blotted up most New York publishers, there had been more focus on profit, less leeway to publish mavericks or material that might not earn much but was worthy of publication, and a steady shrinkage of marginal lines, including mass-market western fiction. At the same time, technology had perfected print-on-demand publication. A book and its cover could be stored in computers, and printed whenever copies were wanted. Warehousing was no longer needed. That in turn gave rise to a new breed of vanity press typified by iUniverse and Xlibris and PublishAmerica, which were not really publishers at all, but printers. They could swiftly produce something that looked like a book for very little cash. These "books" had only rarely been edited or copyedited, had not been adequately proofread, and had undergone no refinement. The whole publishing world was shifting to a new plane, it seemed.

There were democratic and anti-elitist rationalizations

offered for all this: self-publishing was a populist response to a snobby New York establishment that was no longer responsive to the nation's literary tastes. It is true that once in a while a fine book emerges from the world of the self-published and the vanity presses. I think in particular of two friends. One of these, Stanley Gordon West, wrote a powerful novel called *Amos* back in the early eighties. It was the story of an old man in a nursing home fighting its powerful and sinister administration. It soon was turned into an Emmy-nominated TV drama starring Kirk Douglas and Elizabeth Montgomery. And then a funny thing happened. Stan West could never get back on board. He wrote novel after novel, only to have New York publishers bounce them back. He moved from one powerful agent to another, and they could do nothing for him.

Eventually he formed his own publishing company, Lexington-Marshall, and began publishing his own novels in trade paper form. He wrote several richly textured and nostalgic stories about high school students in the 1940s, and then wrote one called *Blind Your Ponies*, about a basketball team from a Montana high school so small that could not even field a full-sized squad. That one was swiftly optioned for film, and eventually Stan sold the rights for a handsome price. He struggled for years, but eventually built his company into a success, and now sells his own novels in large numbers, wins great reviews, and has a following. He makes a considerable income from his books and his company.

Another is my friend Richard Jensen, a Gulf Coast lawyer with great skills as a novelist and nonfiction writer. He wrote some excellent fiction, couldn't sell it to established publishers, and finally had iUniverse produce it. Then he wrote a biography of Tom Mix, digging deep into areas never examined by previous biographers, and eventually produced what surely will be the standard work on the actor. *The Amazing Tom Mix* is excellently edited, copyedited and proofread, and makes an attractive package. It, too, was published by iUniverse because of the lack of interest in it from commercial publishers.

But Stan West and Richard Jensen are exceptions, the one in a thousand self-published people who richly deserve commercial publication. I include their stories as a way of acknowledging that an occasional gifted author can self-publish a work of great merit. But the vast majority of the self-published are far removed from the standards upheld by traditional commercial and academic publishing houses.

There is a clause in the WWA constitution permitting the executive board to admit to membership anyone who has made a valuable contribution to the literature of the West but who doesn't otherwise qualify, and I have always believed that mechanism is the proper one for admitting gifted self-published people to membership. But the organization instead chose an end-run around its organic law. Eventually a change in the bylaws legitimized the practice, and now WWA admits to associate membership self-published and vanity-published writers, as well as writers of unpaid short material. I was dismayed by all that, and so were several other senior members, all Wister Award-winners, but by the time we drafted a letter of protest, the issue was moot.

The swift and systematic doubling of membership made WWA eligible to receive pooled funds collected in Europe from photocopying fees. These funds are distributed by the Authors Coalition of America, a nonprofit corporation devoted to transmitting them to eligible writing groups. To qualify for the funds, an organization has to have at least five hundred professional members whose works are distributed abroad. The coalition also requires that self-published authors in its member organizations must have sold at least a thousand copies and be distributed abroad. With six hundred members, WWA managed to qualify and now receives more funds from this source annually than it does from membership dues. It is affluent, but few of its members are professional writers.

In recent years the organization has expanded the number of Spur Awards to sixteen, and now its awards exceed those of any other genre literature society. (The huge Mystery Writers of America is second, with twelve.) One can also see the direction the WWA board of directors is going in its authorization of a new Spur award for western music. If writing fiction about the West continues to decline, the organization will evolve into something else entirely. My preference is to maintain the value of the awards. In 1987, WWA discontinued its Spur Award for historical novels on the ground that there were too few entries, and it had become a "cheap Spur." Given today's dearth of western fiction from established trade publishers, I believe it would be appropriate to reduce the number of Spurs in that field to one, and radically cut back the other awards as well. Another difficulty is that the Spur Awards are now judged by less-well-credentialed juries. The influx of nonprofessional members has affected the judging. The Spur Awards have lost so much prestige that book most trade publications no longer bother to publish the winners.

WWA has an excellent executive director, the historian Paul Hutton, and an excellent editor of *The Roundup*, Candy Moulton. And yet it surely is the oddest literary society in the country, presiding over a virtually extinct branch of American literature. The romance writers, the mystery writers, the science fiction writers, the private eye writers, the thriller writers, all represent thriving genres. WWA aggressively markets itself and a few of its authors at bookseller conferences and trade shows, but without significant effect. It is not within the powers of any literary society to affect sales or prestige in any major way, so the wizened little world of the western continues to wither.

WWA may eventually evolve into some sort of wax museum of western literature. The conventions now have their share of people wandering around in costume, as if they were manne-quins. There's one fellow who appears each year gotten up like Wild Bill Hickok. Another dresses in mountain man leathers and gewgaws but no doubt bathes more often than real mountain men. Several get duded up as rhinestone cowboys and cowgirls, full of red spangles and bright green boots that have never seen mud. One or two sport mustachios and dress up in long black frock coats and look like 19th century gamblers. Some show up in Native American garb. I have an awful itch to ask all of them, "Yes, but what do you write?"

And yet the conventions still have value to an old man like me, and that lies in reunions with the friends I've met in WWA, the memories of good times, the delight in meeting new and upcoming people, and the simple pleasure of seeing a half-century-old writing society keep on going.

The world belongs to the young, and the young have taken WWA their own direction. It is time to let the next generations do whatever they think best. I will stay on. Western Writers of America gave me my literary career and I am indebted to it. More than that, I love it.

21

The Long Twilight

August, 2006. I've just contracted with a friend to paint my garage. It needs it. The old paint is peeling and cancerous. We still live by small-town standards here. I didn't negotiate a price or a schedule. He will do an excellent job and charge me reasonably. A young lady I know is hanging some rain gutters, fixing fence, replacing faucet gaskets, and will apply a masonry cap to a brick sill that the sun and rain eroded away. Old houses, like old bodies, take a lot of maintenance. I would have done many of these things myself not long ago, but now I can't. We all know abstractly that age brings debility, but it doesn't become real until we actually feel our bodies fail us. Then we know. I have a weakened left ventricle that sometimes betrays me, along with other debilities. I climbed a ladder the other day to do some work on that rain gutter, and retreated, dizzy and sick. The hard lesson is that I must rely on help. And for that I am grateful to live here, where there still are invisible bonds tying people together.

I have work to do, for I cannot abandon my writing. In spite of my best efforts I didn't salt away enough in my IRAs to retire on. So I have a contract to do a biographical novel about John Charles Frémont and Jessie Benton Frémont, and once more I will be examining the life of a man wounded by controversy, a man court-martialed and convicted by the army, a man who ran for the presidency and lost, and a magnificent woman who transformed him into a national hero and took no credit for it and loved him in spite of his betrayals of her.

There is already a fine biographical novel, *Dream West* by David Nevin, but Tom Doherty, who suggested the idea, wanted to see what I could do with Frémont. That is the sort of thing that makes Doherty unique among American publishers. He, more than anyone else who publishes popular fiction, carries within him that literary instinct I've always associated with Scribners and Maxwell Perkins. He reads some of the output of his company, which also is rare. So I will begin that novel when I finish this memoir. I will have a year to complete it and will welcome the slower pace after writing two or three novels a year for almost a quarter of a century. And after that I will write one more Skye's West, and perhaps that will complete the series. My wise counselor Dale Walker cautions me not to write about Skye's death in that last novel. Let him live to see another day. Barnaby Skye has somehow become my doppelganger, and as long as I live, so shall he.

After that, who knows? I wrote a mystery a while ago, and it is still floating about unpurchased. Maybe I will try another.

As I obtain reversions, I put the stories back into print. Fifteen of my novels have gone into the Authors Guild's back-in-print program, and have received dignified packaging and publication. I have just contracted with the savvy people at Sunstone

Press, in Santa Fe, to put another nine of my novels back into print. One of the blessings of these times is that novels need not die; they can be kept alive in giant computers, and a fresh copy can be burped out of a print-on-demand machine at any time. That is a comfort that authors of times gone by didn't have. These reprints don't earn much: the comfort lies in the knowledge that they live, are available, and might enjoy a second life some day. If there should be a revival of interest in an author, there the titles are, readily available.

Most of my novels were original mass market paperbacks, printed on pulp paper that steadily yellows, oxidizes and turns brittle. A mass market book doesn't last, and neither have my stories lasted. The mass market books tumble into dustbins and are thrown out. They offered a brief entertainment and were soon forgotten. The hardcovers have vanished also, some into bookstalls, others into landfill. The physical decay of books forms a good metaphor for my contribution to literature. None of my stories will outlast me; none made any list of notable books. None hold much promise of entertaining future generations. None have caught the interest of academics or historians of literature. It's not that they were bad; it's that they were not timeless and transcending or lyrical.

When I sought to put some of them into print-on-demand editions, I had to scour the used-book markets for copies. When Forge put some of my early Barnaby Skye novels into print-on-demand format, it could not supply copies of its own published novels for scanning, and relied on me to dig up used ones from booksellers. How swiftly stories come and go, stories with transitory appeal to one small segment of the human race, for one brief moment, and then they vanish. And yet there is a small miracle in them: for three decades these little stories have partially or entirely sustained me, put bread on my table, and kept me warm. That is reward enough for me, and the ongoing marvel of my life.

I am changing now. In the past I would begin writing very early, often before dawn. I usually arise around five, and caffeinate myself with some good French Roast, until I have my wits about me. But now I delay. I take my morning walk, ritually following the same path that takes me through the downtown, past the Northern Pacific Beanery, the Livingston Bar and Grille, the Stockman and the Mint (many small Montana towns had their Stockmen and Mint saloons), past Sax and Fryer book store and stationer, Gateway office supply store, and past a Frank Lloyd Wright-designed house now owned by Margot Kidder. I walk past the mansion on the corner of Yellowstone, past the Episcopal, Lutheran and Methodist churches, to my old redbrick house. Some days it is too hot for that, and some days too icy, and some days too windy. We bless our harsh winds; they drive away home buyers and developers. We bless the mean winters, which keep our area rural. We will keep our small town if we can.

One afternoon a few years ago a neighbor rapped on my window and motioned me to the door.

"You have a moose in your back yard," he said.

"Sure, Dan," I replied. But he insisted I look, and sure enough there was the moose. And more recently there was unmistakable bear scat in my yard, about the time the Jonathan apples were dropping. A neighbor lady took a dim view of that.

I have learned to procrastinate. I play the Hearts game on my computer while I wait for the few remaining brain cells in my head to start rowing in unison. I changed the default players to Wyatt, Doc, and Bat, but I beat them regularly because they have a chip for a brain. When I am ready to write, I usually know what I will be saying. I have no ritual. Every day is different. I have no tricks of the trade, either. I don't do as Hemingway did, quit in the middle of a scene or a chapter so that he knew what he would write the next day. It works, but I prefer to write until my brain is fried, and then I quit. I rarely write into the late afternoons. I am a morning person. I reserve the evenings for a good bourbon and water, or a trip to the Bar and Grille to imbibe with friends. I avoid television, but listen to Frank's Place on satellite radio when I am driving. Frank Sinatra sweetly stamped my world, and my 20th Century, so I listen to his world and call it mine. I am privileged to have grown up with real music.

Yesterday I was at a garden party in Paradise Valley given by my friends Keith Lawrie and Patricia Brant Robey. She operates a small publishing company called Fandango Press and is a horsewoman and a director of the animal shelter. He is a poet and musician and bon vivant and hiker and aficionado of great and lovely women. He owns the old farmhouse up Deep Creek where Tom McGuane once lived. There were all sorts of people at the garden party. It was catered by my friends Carole and Dan Sullivan. Dan was a friend of Ed Abbey. We talked about how Dan met Doug Peacock, the "Hayduke" of Abbey's writings, in Glacier Park. Jim and Linda Harrison were at a table along with Marian Hjortsberg. They were stealing a new grandchild named Silas from one another. The child is loaded with writer-genes.

I talked with Alston Chase, who told me his agent loves his new book about Jack Russell Terriers and the animals the Chases have nurtured and the Montana countryside they have owned and nurtured. I visited with Buzz Basini, who has read my entire oeuvre. He is lending my books three at a time to a neighbor. Russell Chatham was there and told me about getting his lithographic press up and running again. I gossiped with my lively next-door neighbor, Joanne Gardner. She ended up in Livingston after abandoning her position as director of the musical video division of Sony.

Glenn Godward, unanimously known as the best bartender in the world, was there as a guest. Dink Bruce was there too. He lives at seventeen feet above sea level in Key West and summers here at four thousand five hundred feet. He is a sort of unofficial mayor of Key West, where he boats and fishes and photographs and paints. He did a swift, bright oil portrait of me, from a snapshot taken across a picnic bench while I was talking to Margot Kidder. It hangs in my study. His parents, Toby and Betty Bruce, were among Ernest Hemingway's friends. Dink gave me a memento, an envelope addressed to Hemingway at Box 406, Key West, Florida. It was from Zane Grey out in Altadena, California. It was mailed on March 20th, 1935, eight days after I was born. It bears an air mail stamp and an air mail sticker. I have it on my mantel, next to my Wister Award bronze buffalo. Dink has a trove of Hemingway memorabilia. After Hemingway died, Dink's mother and Mary Hemingway sorted through stuff Hemingway had stored in the rear room of a Key West watering hole. Mrs. Hemingway took what she wanted and left the rest to the Bruces. The legend of how Dink got his nickname is this: one day when Ernest Hemingway was visiting the Bruces, he saw the baby scoot across the floor, and said, "Look at that little dink go." And the name stuck. But now Dink tells me it's not true. The legend is better than the reality.

I told people I was writing a memoir, and said it would sell about three books. They all disagreed, and thought it might sell four or five. No one in Livingston reads westerns if he can help it. I live in a literary community that has no other novelist of the West except for Diane Smith who has written two fine Viking novels, one about dinosaur hunters on the Missouri river and the other about a woman scientist in early Yellowstone Park. But she's moving to Missoula. Over in Big Timber, Tom McGuane makes sport of modern Montanans, which could be considered western writing. In Livingston, the real scribblers write more glamorous stuff about grizzly bears and ecoterrorists and swimming at the North Pole.

I wish Sue could have come, but she's had some health setbacks and was in Billings. When we married we hoped for a few good years, and we have had them, but things change. She was stricken by a cruel case of shingles in 2004. The disease took a rare turn and settled in her right leg, damaging the motor nerves that govern her right foot. She needs a four-prong cane now. That illness didn't stop her from accompanying me back to my birthplace in Wisconsin, where my high school honored me on its "Wall of Inspiration" in April of 2005. In Milwaukee I got to introduce my bride to several of my family who had never met her, including my cousins, my brother Tim, and my new sister-in-law Shermane Billingsley. I am the exotic member of my family, the macaw in a family of robins, but they all collected in Milwaukee to celebrate the honor. None cares much about the American West or western fiction but some of them had proudly bought my every novel and kept up with my writing life, and quietly supported me in every imaginable way, and I look back upon these gifts as treasures. I have never been alone.

Sue and I talk between four and five each afternoon, and that is our diurnal communion, except that we are one hundred fifteen miles apart and I don't greet her with a kiss, or see her smile. For most of my marriage Sue has been a voice on the telephone. That is the union we fashioned, and that's how it will play out. But there is always the next rendezvous.

My death is not far away now. I do not know what lies beyond the grave, if anything. So I have invented my own eternity. In my blue heaven, only love is eternal. Love carries us into the life to come, beyond the beyond. When we love someone, we vest that person with eternity. We fashion our heaven out of our earthly life, and populate it with the ones we have loved. The person who has loved only himself will have only a bare room. But I am among the fortunate, for I have loved deeply and well, and all my beloved ones will be with me, family and friends, the women I have loved, the writers I have esteemed, the pets who came to live with me. My heaven will be full and not at all lonely. And maybe, because I have been loved, I'll be in other heavens too.

Appendix

At one time I was a guest lecturer at a writing workshop in Whitefish, Montana. The students had undergone intensive how-to training in intimate sessions, presided over by some of the best instructors in the business. I knew I would have nothing to add to what these excellent instructors had already taught.

I wondered whether the students might profit from a lecture devoted to the status of American literature and how they might fit into it. With great trepidation—I was certain the talk would be a disaster—I drafted the talk appended here. It turned out to be the most successful talk I've ever given, and his been widely reprinted. Here it is:

I am pleased to be here today. Thank you for coming here and listening to an elderly novelist wend his way along the primrose path.

Writing skills are largely self-taught, but perhaps I can steer you in a new direction, and maybe I will inspire you to try something different and promising. I am hoping to persuade you to look at literature in new ways. I am also hoping that you will find yourself writing more compelling novels and selling them successfully.

What I'm going to say does not seem at all radical to me but it will seem radical to you because it will challenge your understanding of modern literature.

We are all familiar with the idea that there is literary fiction, and there is popular fiction. Most of us choose to write in one realm or the other. Literary fiction is considered the more prestigious form of the novel, the more serious art, and is regarded as a higher calling than popular fiction. Literary fiction is usually defined as the examination of the human condition. The literary novelist sets out to depict the truth in human relationships, and wins acclaim according to how penetrating the novel is. The perception we entertain is that the literary novelist is a person of great education, whose language is disciplined and rich with metaphor and simile and figures of speech, whose work is polished and refined to a level rarely seen in commercial fiction. Literary novels receive the great prizes, such as the Pulitzer, the Nobel, and the National Book Award. Literary fiction is what you master in academic venues such as the famous Iowa Writers Workshop. Literary novels are dutifully studied in thousands of college English classes.

It is easy to see why so many of us seek to write this prestigious fiction, seek its rewards, seek the reviews and serious criticism that envelop this literature. An appreciation of literary fiction is taught on campuses across the country by intelligent academics who want their students to absorb the greatness placed before them.

Popular fiction, on the other hand, is regarded as commerce, factory fiction for a humbler readership, mostly the less-educated. Here plot becomes more important, page-turning tension is vital, characterization and subtlety are sacrificed to the more important business of keeping the story rolling along. There is less space for reflection, and little soul-searching depth in commercial fiction. Popular fiction often transports readers away from the real world whereas literary fiction often carries a reader into the real world, and literary novelists are celebrated for their keen eye.

A popular novel is rarely regarded as a contribution to our literary heritage. Popular fiction ranges from the big commercial novels of skilled authors down to sheer hackwork one occasionally finds in some original mass market paperbacks. Indeed, I believe the very idea of popular fiction rose from the appearance of mass-market paperbacks after World War Two.

Until recently, authors who wrote popular fiction thought it provided a better income than literary fiction. Publishers threw their resources behind blockbuster and midlist novels, and the result was real rewards for the commercial novelist. But times are changing and who can say what the future will bring? I suspect that just now, most literary novelists earn more.

If you have believed in these distinctions, and have believed that the world of fiction has always been divided into these two sharply defined categories, you will be surprised to learn that it probably is not so. The distinction made between literary and popular fiction is quite modern; indeed, it evolved in my own lifetime. Back in the forties and fifties, if you had asked Ernest Hemingway or John Dos Passos or John Steinbeck or James Jones whether he wrote literary or popular fiction, you would probably have gotten a blank stare or a request to define what you mean. Likewise, if you had asked such distinguished publishers as Alfred Knopf or Charles Scribner whether he published literary or commercial fiction, he would have been confounded by the question. For these people, there was simply literature. It might be serious literature or light-hearted literature. It might be genre literature—mysteries and westerns were identified as separate branches of literature. Those publishers produced all sorts of novels. Alfred Knopf proudly published W. R. Burnett, a novelist who wrote westerns as well the classic crime story that brought him fame, *The Asphalt Jungle*. Scribners proudly published S. S. Van Dine, a mystery writer, alongside Hemingway and Tom Wolfe and Marjorie Kinnan Rawlings.

If the distinction between literary and commercial fiction was unknown to authors and publishers, it was also unknown to the Pulitzer Committee in that period. *Gone With the Wind*, by Margaret Mitchell, won a Pulitzer for fiction. So did *The Yearling*, by Margorie Kinnan Rawlings. *Tales of the South Pacific*, by James Michener. *Advise and Consent*, by Allen Drury. *The Way West*, by A. B. Guthrie, Jr. *The Caine Mutiny*, by Herman Wouk, *The Travels of Jaimie McPheeters*, by Robert Lewis Taylor, and *The Grapes of Wrath*, John Steinbeck's masterpiece. These were all simply literature and they all won a Pulitzer.

Most authors and publishers of that period would have told you that good fiction requires *all* the qualities that were later divided between literary and popular fiction. That is, a fine novel does have a compelling storyline with a beginning, middle, and end, page-turning tension, rich characterization, lapidary prose, a consideration of the human condition, a sense of tragedy or comedy, mastery of a milieu, and broad appeal to both well educated and less educated people. Authors of that period prided themselves on the universality of their stories. If they could appeal to college-educated people, fine; if they could appeal to the humblest reader, even better. There was little of the elitism that now attaches to literary fiction. Ernest Hemingway made a point of using words that were universally understood. No reasonably literate reader could possibly have trouble understanding or interpreting a Hemingway novel.

So, the distinction between literary and popular fiction is quite recent, three or four decades old. When I was a youth it didn't exist. Yet today it is a given: we assume that there have always been two branches of literature, and we writers need to make one or the other our own. Where did it come from? I had no idea how it evolved until my friend Win Blevins, who has an advanced degree in criticism from Columbia University, enlightened me. The distinction between literary and popular fiction arose, he told me, about the time when colleges began to offer workshop courses in creative writing, especially in the 1960s and 1970s.

Teachers used the term "literary" to describe what was to be taught in these workshops. These seminars would teach students the art of writing a "serious" novel, and not something light or transitory or appealing to popular tastes. This distinction gradually became the norm, and in modern times "literary fiction" has become a distinct branch of literature that pursues truths about the human condition and is also a vehicle for progressive social comment.

This is tragic. It is well to keep in mind that the novels that endure through the generations, the ones that we call classics, were largely written for ordinary people, not educated elites. Mark Twain and Charles Dickens and Jack London wrote stories intended for all of us. In fact, through most of American literature, both fiction and nonfiction, authors made a point of writing for people in all walks of life. Let me do a roll call of American authors and poets who sought to write for all people: Nathaniel Hawthorne, Herman Melville, Washington Irving, James Fenimore Cooper, Edgar Allan Poe, Henry David Thoreau, Henry Wadsworth Longfellow, Walt Whitman, Carl Sandburg, Robert Frost, James Baldwin. Where is this leading me? To a belief that the whole idea of an elite "literary" fiction is a departure from a deeply-rooted American storytelling tradition that has always been democratic and universal. I believe that American letters has been highjacked by elitists and American fiction has suffered ever since.

Now we live in a world in which New York publishers are sharply divided. Some, such as Viking, Scribners, Alfred Knopf, Farrar, Straus and Giroux, or HarperCollins, devote themselves almost entirely to literary fiction while others, such as St. Martin's, Forge, Doubleday or Simon and Schuster largely devote themselves to popular fiction. And you, the novelists, must decide which direction to go. *The New York Times* and the *New York Review of Books* and *The New Yorker* are largely devoted to reviewing literary works. Only rarely do they review popular fiction, while other publications such as regional newspapers often devote themselves to popular fiction.

I consider this a most unsatisfactory state of affairs. For one thing, I think the dichotomy is false. There is no reason why a popular novel with a dramatic storyline cannot also be a novel that probes the human condition. There is no reason why a literary novel that delves deep into relationships or character cannot also have a storyline that hustles along and compels attention. These false distinctions should be thrown out. A slow and plotless novel is bad writing, no matter whether it is the proper form for literary fiction. A shallow story that moves fast but is devoid of characterization is bad writing no matter whether it is the proper form for popular fiction. I believe that a good story avoids the weaknesses of both:

It moves right along.

It rewards readers.

It illuminates life.

It is time, I think, to discard these distinctions between the two literary forms. And that is what I wish to bring to you this day. We in American literature are prisoners of some assumptions that aren't really valid. I believe this division of fiction into upper and lower tiers is bad for American literature, bad for publishers, bad for authors, bad for booksellers and wholesalers and the reading public. I believe this distinction between literary and popular fiction is a major reason that fiction is in decline and few important literary figures have emerged for the last several decades.

In a remarkable millennial essay written a few years ago, Jonathan Yardley, the Pulitzer Prize-winning critic of *The Washington Post*, whom I regard as the finest reviewer in the country, noted that American literature is in decline, and no truly grand novelists have emerged for several decades. He further noted that the only vitality and originality on the horizon currently rises from genre fiction, especially mysteries. Think about that. Something is plenty wrong with American literature just now. I think I know what it is, and what you, who want a literary career, can do about it.

Above all, I want you to expand your horizons and set sail for something bigger and better than either of the current branches of fiction. I want you to write novels that are larger than anything being written today. I want you to write stories that embrace the best of both worlds. I want you to write stories that are accessible by everyone. Do you want to do something for American fiction? Then write novels that weld the broken pieces back together.

I am a veteran reader of genre fiction and have been skeptical of these distinctions for a long time. I am especially skeptical of the idea that literary fiction is *innately* superior to popular fiction. I have often found imaginative commercial novels that are superbly crafted in all respects: lyrical language, vivid depictions of life, rich explorations of character, finely chiseled sentences that evoke scenes and moods and understandings of our world. I've come to believe that these distinctions so loved by the critics simply fall apart.

I may surprise you now. I try not write popular fiction and I try not write literary fiction. I've written western novels that are published in genre western lines, historical novels published as general fiction, biographical novels also published as popular fiction, and even a contemporary novel set in the West. But not even my genre westerns, pure entertainment fiction you might suppose, really fall into the realm of commercial storytelling. I am always inserting the core values of literary fiction, such as rich characterization and a look at the meaning of what is transpiring, into these stories. Some of my historical novels have a theme, a sure mark of the literary novel. One of them, *Second Lives*, is about people who rebuild their ruined lives in Denver of the 1880s. It was published as "popular" fiction but is really "literary" fiction as these things are currently defined . It certainly doesn't belong on the western shelves along with Max Brand and Luke Short. Actually, not one of my longer historical novels falls into either category, which may make my publishers and reviewers unhappy.

I should add that reviewers don't know how to review my novels because they fit no comfortable niche. But my refusal to live within literary boundaries has enabled me to write a better novel than if I had adhered to the literary forms that critics and publishers impose on us. I begin simply with the idea that a good novel embraces all of the best qualities of literary and commercial fiction, and avoids the weaknesses of either category. I focus on story, and don't care what kind of story or what pigeonhole it might fit into.

This also makes wholesalers and retailers unhappy. How do you categorize a Wheeler novel? Often I find my large-scale historical novels or biographical novels on the same shelves as Louis L'Amour, where they don't belong. I can't help that. As long as American literature remains self-imprisoned by unreal distinctions, and books are shelved according to ironclad categories, there is no help for it. But I think it has been worth the risk, worth the confusion, and I would not go back and write either commercial or literary fiction as they are currently defined. I didn't wholly succeed, and probably hurt my sales by pushing at boundaries and confounding publishing categories, but I have no regrets.

What I propose to you is this: Consider writing stories that embody the best of both literary and commercial fiction. Or to put it another way, see if you can write fiction that avoids the worst of each variety.

Now I will proceed to some of my other bugaboos. I keep coming across authors who ache to be trendy. They want to write a cutting-edge story that heads exactly in the direction of what the Germans call the Zeitgeist, the spirit or trend of the times. Perhaps they think this will win them more attention; more acclaim if they plug into the very thing everyone is absorbed with. I don't know. I do know that you are likely to be imitative if you write a trendy book. You will surrender your sovereignty, your uniqueness, if you want to be trendy. Let me put it this way: James Jones didn't write *From Here to Eternity* because he thought that military stories would be hot stuff in the wake of World War Two. He had a searing, unquenchable need to dramatize his brutal military life.

I worry about young people in these times because so many seem too eager to walk lockstep with their crowd rather than grow in independence. If your wish is to be the acolyte at every altar, then choose another calling. If you are the sort who has a cell phone glued to your ear and a TV turned on wherever you are, you probably should choose another vocation. If you hope to write good literature, you need independence of mind, and that means distancing yourself from the chattering classes, and coming to your own conclusions.

You want to be a novelist. But why? Have you anything to say? The ultimate futility is to write when you have nothing to say.

I know of only two good reasons to write fiction. One is money. Those who say they don't write for money usually aren't able to sell what they write. If someone tells me he or she wants to write fiction to make a lot of money, I will think that is commendable, but naive.

Publishable writing is wrought by hard work—often difficult, usually time-consuming. It requires a real mastery of art and craft that can't be won overnight. It takes trial and error. There will be disappointments. If you aspire to the role of a professional writer, your intent is to reach a wide audience, and the only way to do this is through publishing what you have written. But remember this: publishers of books and periodicals also aspire to success. Your publishers want your novel to sell well; that is how they make money, and how they pay you royalties. Sales are the acid test: if your book sells well, it usually means you have written something commendable. That is not always true; junk stories sometimes sell. But you would be wise to write for money and hope for good sales and to consider your literary vocation a business like any other business. A good sale says a great deal about the merit of your work.

You need to have something to say and something worth saying. If you tell me you simply want to be a writer but give me no rationale for your ambition, I will think your chances of success are poor. But if you tell me you are passionately interested in, say, the history of Montana ranching, and want to get your ideas and research into readable book form, I will think your chances of becoming a writer are excellent.

How do you know whether you have anything to say? The best clue is your curiosity. If you are naturally curious about the world, curious about how things work, how things happen, how anything came into being, then the chances are that you have something within you to write about. If you absorb the world as it is and ask few questions and never let your mind roam toward answers, chances are you have little to say. If your mind is the sort that pursues questions, then your odds of becoming a successful writer are very good indeed.

Let me turn now to the single most important element of any novel. When people ask me what makes a good or even great novel, or a marketable novel, I tell them three things: story, story, and story. My idea of a great story may not be your idea of one so I won't list examples. Instead, I will suggest what great stories have within them. You have heard that stories must have conflict in them, but that old cliché is inadequate. Stories are about dilemma. Your protagonist has a dilemma to resolve, and sometimes that multiplies into many dilemmas. Really good stories involve a dilemma that tests the character of the protagonist, that challenges the beliefs of people, that probes right and wrong, good and evil. Because good stories pose dilemmas, they must also pose a resolution to the dilemma. In other words, a good novel has an ending, even if a tragic ending. Great stories are set in moral contexts; a story built on nihilist premises usually falls flat. Great stories are magical.

Here I can go no further. I can't tell you how to write great stories. I really don't know how myself. But your future as a novelist depends on your ability to spin a magical story. Not so much on your basic writing skills, not so much on your dialogue or characterization, not on your vocabulary, not even on your sophistication. But on the magical power and grace of your stories.

To sum up: write something that won't fit into the pigeonholes of literature imposed by reviewers and critics. Write for money. Write because you have something to say, and not because you want to be a writer. Avoid the trendy, choosing instead to follow your own counsel. And focus on story above all else. None of this will guarantee you success, but all of it will improve your chances.

Literary Credits

Published or Contracted Fiction as of January 2007

General:

Bushwack, western fiction, Doubleday, 1978. British edition, Robert Hale, London.

Beneath the Blue Mountain, western fiction, Doubleday, 1979. British edition, Robert Hale, London.

Winter Grass, western fiction, Walker and Company, 1983. Finalist for the Spur Award for best western novel, Western Writers of America. Large print edition, Thorndike. Paperback edition, Ballantine, May, 1986. Library of Congress talking book. Audio edition, August, 2002, Books in Motion.

Sam Hook, western fiction, Walker and Company, 1986. Large type edition, Thorndike. Ballantine paperback, August, 1987. British edition, Robert Hale, London. Books in Motion Audio Edition, March, 2003. Sunstone Press trade paperback, 2008

Richard Lamb, western fiction. Walker and Company, 1987. Ballantine paperback edition, September, 1988. Books in Motion Audio Edition, March, 2003. Sunstone Press trade paperback, 2008.

Dodging Red Cloud, western fiction, M. Evans and Co., 1987. Ballantine paperback, January, 1989. Large print edition, Nightingale, 1989. Audio Book, Recorded Books, Inc., 1991.

Stop, western fiction, M. Evans and Co., 1988. Ballantine paperback, July, 1989. Large print edition, Thorndike. British edition, Robert Hale, London. Audio book, Books in Motion, 2004.

Fool's Coach, western fiction, M. Evans and Co., April, 1989. Winner of the Spur Award for Best Western Novel of 1989. Large type edition, Thorndike, including British rights. Tor paperback edition, July, 1991. Audio Book, Territory Titles, A Pegasus Western, 1995. Books in Motion, unabridged audio on CD, May, 2005.

Where the River Runs, western fiction, M. Evans and Co., February, 1990. Large print edition, Thorndike. Tor paperback edition, January, 1992. Audio book, Recorded Books, Inc., 1992. South Korean edition, Hong Ik Publishing Co., Seoul, 1993. Finalist for the Spur Award, 1990.

Montana Hitch, western fiction, M. Evans and Co., October, 1990. Tor paperback edition, December, 1992. Thorndike large type edition, 1991.

Badlands, historical novel of the west dealing with fossil hunters, 125,000 words, Tor Books, 1992. Tor's lead book for August. Major promotion: posters, three author tours. Re-released June, 1994. Print-on-demand trade paperback edition, Ingram, November, 2000. Audio edition: Books in Motion, May, 2006. Sunstone Press trade edition, 2008.

The Two Medicine, Rivers West series, Taneycomo Productions. Bantam Books, May, 1993. Audio edition, Books in Motion, 2000.

Cashbox, a 150,000-word saga of a silver mining town, Forge Books, June, 1994. Forge paperback edition, April, 1995. Large print edition, G. K. Hall, 1996. Finalist for the Spur Award for Best Novel of the West.

Goldfield, a 150,000-word saga of a gold mining town and a companion book to *Cashbox*. Forge hardcover April, 1995; paperback publication April, 1996. Large print edition, Thorndike, 1996. Hardcover, World Publishers Promotions.

Sierra, a 160,000-word 1849 gold rush saga and love story. Forge hardcover publication September, 1996. Large print edition, Thorndike, 1997. Winner of the Spur Award for Best Novel of the West published in 1996. Paperback edition August, 1998.

Second Lives, a 150,000-word novel of the Gilded Age, set in Denver in the 1880s. Forge hardcover, May, 1997. Mass market edition, March, 1999.

The Buffalo Commons, a contemporary drama, 150,000 words, pitting a Montana ranch family rooted to the land against those who would like to depopulate eastern Montana and return it to buffalo pasture. Forge hardcover, March, 1998. Mass Market, April, 2000. Thorndike large print hardcover, 1999.

Aftershocks, a 150,000-word novel of the San Francisco earthquake and fire of 1906, Forge hardcover, January, 1999. Mass market edition, October, 1999.

Sun Mountain, a 150,000-word novel about Virginia City, Nevada, and Mark Twain. Forge hardcover. May, 1999. Mass market edition, August, 2002. Sunstone Press trade paperback edition, 2008.

Masterson, a biographical novel about frontier lawman Bat Masterson, focusing on his life in New York. Forge hardcover, 100,000 words. October, 1999. Author tour. Winner of the Spur Award for Best Western Novel published in 1999. Mass market edition, June, 2000. Large print edition, Center Point, March, 2001.

The Fields of Eden, 150,000-word historical novel about the settlement of Oregon, Forge Books, May, 2001. Mass market edition, January, 2003. Sunstone Press trade paperback edition, 2008.

The Exile, An Irish Rebel in America, biographical novel about Governor Thomas Francis Meagher, Forge Books. Hardcover, December, 2003.

Eclipse, a biographical novel about Meriwether Lewis and William Clark after they return, Forge Books, May, 2002. Forge trade paperback edition, September, 2003.

Cutthroat Gulch, a traditional 75,000-word western novel for Signet, New American Library, April, 2003.

An Obituary for Major Reno, a biographical novel about Major Marcus Reno, Forge Books, hardcover, December, 2004, Forge mass market, December, 2005.

Trouble in Tombstone, a biographical novel about Wyatt Earp, Signet/ NAL, December, 2004.

The Honorable Cody, a biographical novel about Buffalo Bill Cody, Sunstone Press, Original trade paper, October, 2006.

John Charles and Jessie Benton Fremont novel, Forge, unscheduled.

Skye's West series for Tor/Forge. These are 95,000-word novels about a guide and his Indian family in the pre-settlement western wilderness.

Sun River, Skye's West series, Tor, July, 1989. Tom Doherty Associates trade paperback, 2002

Bannack, Skye's West series, Tor, October, 1989. Thorndike hardcover large print edition, 2000. Tom Doherty Associates trade paperback, 2002

The Far Tribes, Skye's West series, Tor, March, 1990. Finalist for the Spur Award for Best Novel of the West, 1990. Tom Doherty Associates trade paperback, 2002.

Yellowstone, Skye's West series, Tor, October, 1990. Tom Doherty Associates trade paperback, 2002.

Bitterroot, Skye's West series, Tor, August, 1991. Tom Doherty Associates trade paperback, 2003.

Sundance, Skye's West series, Tor, October, 1992. Tom Doherty Associates trade paperback, 2002.

Wind River, Skye's West series, Tor, August, 1993. Tom Doherty Associates trade paperback, 2002.

Santa Fe, Skye's West series, Tor/Forge, November, 1994. Tom Doherty Associates trade paperback, 2003.

Rendezvous, Skye's West Series, Tor/Forge 80,000-word hardcover, December, 1997. Mass market edition, December, 1998. Thorndike hardcover large print edition, 1998.

Dark Passage, Skye's West series, Tor/Forge hardcover, November, 1998. Mass market September, 2000. Large print hardcover, Center Point Publishing

Going Home, Skye's West series, Tor/Forge hardcover, December, 2000. Mass market edition, 2001. Large print trade paper, Wheeler Publishing Co. (No relation.)

Downriver, Skye's West series, Forge hardcover, December, 2001. Starred lead review in *Publishers Weekly*. Doubleday Book Club and The Literary Guild selection.

The Deliverance, Skye's West series, Forge hardcover, March, 2003.

The Fire Arrow, Skye's West number 14, Forge hardcover, 80,000 words, May, 2006.

Canyon of Bones, Skye's West number 15, Forge hardcover, 80,000 words, April, 2007.

Virgin River, Skye's West number 16, Forge hardcover, unscheduled

Skye's West number 17, Forge hardcover, unscheduled.

A series of 60,000-word paperback originals first published by Ballantine and Fawcett, and now in trade paperback from Sunstone Press, featuring Santiago Toole, doctor-sheriff at Miles City, Montana Territory.

Incident at Fort Keogh, a Santiago Toole novel, Ballantine, July, 1990. Thorndike large type edition, 1991. Audio book, Sunset Productions, 1993. Sunstone Press trade paperback edition, 2007.

The Final Tally, Santiago Toole series, Fawcett, February, 1991. Re-released in low priced edition, 1993. Thorndike large type edition, 1992. Audio book, Sunset Productions, 1994. Sunstone Press trade paperback edition, 2007.

Deuces and Ladies Wild, Santiago Toole series, Fawcett, July, 1991. Re-released, 1993. Thorndike large type edition, 1992. Audio book, Sunset Productions, 1993. Sunstone Press trade paperback edition, 2007.

The Fate, Santiago Toole series, Fawcett, June, 1992. Re-released, 1993 and 1999. Audio book, Sunset Productions, 1994. Sunstone Press trade paperback edition, 2007.

A three-book series called *The Rocky Mountain Company* for Pinnacle/ Zebra, running 100,000 words and featuring three families in the buffalo robe trade in the 1840s.

The Rocky Mountain Company, Pinnacle, March, 1991. Reprint, June, 2002. Large print edition, Wheeler Publishing Co. (No relation.) August, 2002. Adobe E-book.

Fort Dance, Pinnacle, November, 1991. Reprint, September, 2002. Large Print Edition, Thorndike, 2003.

Cheyenne Winter, Pinnacle, April, 1992. Reprint, November, 2002

A series about a frontier newspaper editor named Sam Flint; 80,000-word novels.

Flint's Truth, Forge Books, hardcover, May, 1998, mass market, October, 2000. Audio rights: Blackstone Audio Book, Recorded Books. G. K. Hall large print, 1998.

Flint's Gift, Forge Books, hardcover, September, 1997, mass market June, 1999. Audio rights: Blackstone Audio Books, Recorded Books., 1998. Large print edition, G. K. Hall, 1998.

Flint's Honor, Forge Books, hardcover, July, 1999, mass market, March, 2001. Audio rights: Blackstone Audio Books, Recorded Books. Large print, G. K. Hall, 2001.

The Witness Series, a three-book contract with NAL/Dutton for 75,000-word Westerns in which the protagonists face moral or ethical dilemmas, or crises of conscience.

The Witness, NAL/Dutton, July, 2000. Spur Award finalist, Best Western Novel, 2001.

Restitution, NAL/Dutton, February, 2001. Large Print, Gale Group, October, 2001. Spur Award finalist, Best Western Novel, 2002.

Drum's Ring, NAL/Dutton, July, 2001; Large Print, Gale Group, March, 2002. Winner of the Spur Award for Best Original Paperback, Western Writers of America, 2002.

Mining Camp Series for Pinnacle/Zebra:

Bounty Trail, Pinnacle, a mining camp story, February, 2004.

Vengeance Valley, a mining camp story, Pinnacle, September, 2004. Winner of the Spur Award for Best Original Paperback.

Seven Miles to Sundown, a mining camp story, Pinnacle, April, 2005

Fire in the Hole, a mining camp story, Pinnacle, September, 2005.

From Hell to Midnight, a mining camp story, Pinnacle, April, 2006

Short stories:

"The Business of Dying," *The Morrow Anthology of Great Western Short Stories*, edited by Jon Tuska and Vicki Piekarski, William Morrow, 1997.

"A Fate Worse Than Death," audio anthology, edited by Robert Randisi. *How the West Was Read, II*, Durkin Hayes, December, 1997.

"The Last Days of Dominic Prince," *American West: Twenty New Stories from the Western Writers of America*, edited by Loren D. Estleman, Forge Books, January, 2001. Finalist for the Spur Award, best short story, Western Writers of America.

"Hearts," in *Stagecoach*, a Tombstone anthology, edited by Ed Gorman, Berkley, September, 2003. Reprint, Best Stories of the American West, Vol. 1, scheduled early 2007.

"The Tinhorn's Lady," August, 2000, Readthewest.com.

"Dead Weight," *Boot Hill* anthology, Robert Randisi, editor, Forge, May, 2002.

"A Commercial Proposition," *White Hats* anthology, Robert Randisi, Berkley, July, 2002.

"The Square Reporter," in *Westward, A fictional History of the American West*, Dale Walker, ed., June, 2003.

Editor:

Tales of the American West, The Best of Spur Award-Winning Authors, Richard S. Wheeler, Editor, New American Library, September, 2000. Mass market edition, June, 2001. Hardcover large print edition, May, 2001., Wheeler Publishing Co. (No relation.)

Printed in the United States
89038LV00005B/168/A

9 780865 345638